Editor
Lorin Klistoff, M.A.

Editor in Chief
Karen J. Goldfluss, M.S. Ed.

Cover Artist
Marilyn Goldberg

Illustrator
Teacher Created Resources

Art Manager
Kevin Barnes

Imaging
Craig Gunnell
James Edward Grace

Publisher
Mary D. Smith, M.S. Ed.

WORLD HISTORY

Grades 5-8

READERS' THEATER

Bringing the past to life!

- Original scripts based on historic events and highlights
- Introductory background information to set the stage for each script
- Reader's response and extension activities
- Convenient, reproducible pull-out scripts for each student

Teacher Created Resources

Author

Robert W. Smith

Teacher Created Resources, Inc.
12621 Western Avenue
Garden Grove, CA 92841
www.teachercreated.com

ISBN: 978-1-4206-3998-8

©2008 Teacher Created Resources, Inc.
Reprinted, 2019
Made in U.S.A.

Teacher Created Resources

TABLE OF CONTENTS

TABLE OF CONTENTS

INTRODUCTION

What is Readers' Theater?

Readers' theater is drama without the need for costumes, props, stage, or memorization. It is performed in the classroom by groups of students who become the cast of the dramatic reading. The players employ their oral reading skills, creative expression, and dramatic voice to communicate the mood and the meaning of the script. Students should have practiced the script several times over a few days and be well versed in the meaning of the text and well practiced in using correct pronunciation, proper voice inflection, appropriate changes in volume, and various nuances of expression to create an effective dramatic reading. They should also understand the historical context of the readings.

Why Use Readers' Theater in Social Studies?

Children need to live history. A steady diet of textbook readings and vague focus questions tend to make history a series of meaningless, disconnected events. The vibrant story of our recorded human history becomes dry, tasteless, and boring. Students need to have a sense of involvement with the human dramas that make up the history of men and women all through the ages.

They can imagine the excitement of seeing unknown lands, dynamic human societies, and exotic wildlife as Marco Polo and Captain James Cook did. They can get a glimpse of the extraordinary creativity and imagination of Leonardo da Vinci, Isaac Newton, and the Impressionist painters.

Children will understand the motivations, struggles, and concerns of individuals caught up in the chaos and terror of revolutionary events. They should be both astonished and disturbed by the clash of cultures during the conquest of Mexico by Cortés and the conflicts between Captain Cook and the Polynesian peoples he met. They will be stunned by the immediacy of death in times of plague, revolution, and conquest. Using readers' theater and other dramatic activities is a creative way to grab students' imagination and focus it on a period of history.

Literature Connections

The stories that unfold in these readers' theater scripts can be the spark that spurs student interest in some of the best children's historical literature and biography. Biographies of Newton, Leonardo, Vincent Van Gogh, Mary Cassatt, and Elizabeth I escort a child into the minds and motivations of scientists, artists, and public leaders. Tales of exploration and adventure create a vehicle to bring children along for the ride with Captain Cook, Hernando Cortés, or Marco Polo. Each unit in this book highlights an effective and engaging piece of children's literature to help you extend the lesson.

Writing Dramatic History

Children become more involved in historical events when they immerse themselves in the action. Having children create scripts based on the historical epochs they are studying is a good way of developing students who think about historical events and consider the consequences of individual human actions and cultural interactions. Encourage your students to use the dramatic format and the suggestions in each extension activity to create their own readers' theater scripts.

Use the discussion activities on the last page of each unit to help students internalize the motives of the characters in the scripts or to draw closure after the script has been performed.

Targeting the Topics

You will want to use the scripts in this book as you teach individual units of world history. There are representative scripts for periods beginning with the Middle Ages and the explorations of Marco Polo through the Nazi launch of the Holocaust. In this span are topics as diverse as the Age of Exploration, the rise of modern science, the eruptions of revolutionary change, massive political upheavals, and monumental clashes between cultures.

Working with the Scripts

Each script is designed to illuminate one facet or significant event in the historical sweep of a given era. The background information preceding each script gives a brief historical context to help your students place the event in terms of time and place. Depending upon circumstances, you may want to do several scripts simultaneously with your class as you finish a semester of work or do the scripts along the way as you finish individual topics in world history. Teachers whose time for teaching history in the upper elementary grades is limited may choose to use these scripts and the background information as the primary vehicle for social studies instruction and reinforce these tools with selected textbook readings or high quality historical fiction in children's literature. (**Note to Teacher:** It is important to review the content of each script prior to classroom study. Choose scripts that are appropriate to your curriculum and are suitable for your students.)

Selecting Teams and Leaders

If all of your class will be doing readers' theater dramatic readings, select good readers and effective leaders for key roles in each script. These leaders will often do the narration or provide a strong voice for one of the longer or more important dramatic parts. They should help resolve some questions of pronunciation and the meanings for words that are unfamiliar to some of the students. You will also need to assist teams with these tasks and resolve occasional disputes related to meaning or role selection.

Selecting Teams and Leaders (cont.)

Assign each of the student script leaders a team composed of students with varying reading ability. You may want shy children, struggling readers, or students just learning English to have more limited roles in their first readers' theater experiences. However, all students should have ample time to practice with their fellow team members so that the performance is effective and interesting to the student audience.

Staging

Your classroom is the stage. Place the proper number (four to seven) of stools, chairs, or desks to sit on in a semicircle at the front of your class or in a separate staging area. You may use simple costumes, but generally no costume is expected or used in this type of dramatization. If you have plain robes or simple coats of the same color or style so that everyone looks about the same, this can have a nice effect. Students dressed in the same school uniform or colors create an atmosphere of seriousness. Props are not needed, but they may be used for additional effects.

Scripting

Each member of your group should have a clearly marked, usable script, as well as the complete unit with background information, extensions, and discussion questions. Students should be able to personalize the script with notes indicating when they speak, which part or parts they are reading, and mechanical notes about pronunciation of specific words and phrases or sentences they intend to emphasize in some dramatic way.

Performing

Students should enter the classroom quietly and seriously. They should sit silently and unmoving on the stools or chairs. Performers should wait with heads lowered, or they should focus on an object above the audience. When the narrator starts the reading, the actors can then focus on whoever is reading, except when they are performing.

Movement, Memorization, and Mime

Experienced readers' theater actors may add gestures or other movements to their lines. Some actors may choose to introduce mime to a performance if it seems to fit. Several actors will learn their lines so well that they have virtually memorized them. Some students will want to add props or costumes, as the circumstances allow. More involved actors often begin to add accents to a character in the script.

Assessment

Base performance assessments on the pacing, volume, expression, and focus of the participants. Student-authored scripts should demonstrate general writing skills, dramatic tension, and a good plot. Class discussions should reflect serious thought, use of the background information, and references to the text of the script.

READERS' THEATER

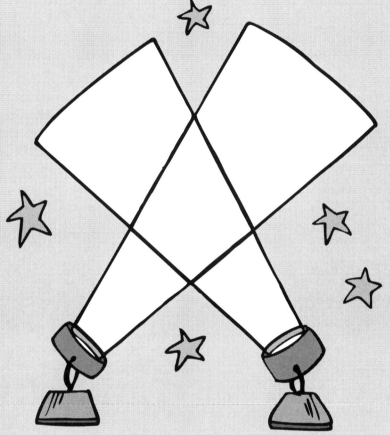

MARCO MILLIONS

BACKGROUND: MARCO MILLIONS

The Travels of Marco Polo

In 1271, Niccolo and Maffeo Polo decided to return to China accompanied by Niccolo's 17-year-old son, Marco. The two experienced traders saw that Marco was strong and eager to make the journey to the court of Kublai Khan where the brothers had already spent one year. The journey through Asia took more than three and one-half years and was filled with danger. They traveled through the Caucausus Mountains, across Persia and Armenia, through high passes in the Pamir Mountains, and across the Gobi desert.

Marco kept careful journals of all the wonders he saw and the stories he heard. Some of the stories he heard from traders and natives may have been entirely or mostly fiction, but his observations have generally been proven correct. Oil does seep from the earth in some parts of Asia, and people had learned to use it to treat the mange, a skin disease in animals, and for lighting lamps. The hard, black burning stones he saw were coal.

The stories he told of China's wonders and the palaces of Kublai Khan were largely true, although he might have exaggerated some to stress the great wealth and importance of China. They did have paper money, a pony express system for sending messages, and the Chinese did bathe frequently, an idea that seemed strange to Europeans who rarely bathed. Marco described animals that had never been known in Europe before, such as the crocodile and the rhinoceros.

Marco Polo worked as a governor of a province and an observer for Kublai Khan, who trusted him and admired his observations and judgments. The emperor did not want the Polos to leave China, and they stayed there for 17 years before he allowed them to go as ambassadors for him, delivering a princess as a bride for a Persian king.

MARCO POLO

The Polos weren't even recognized in Venice or their own home when they returned. They held a party for their friends and tore their clothes into which they had sewn jewels and gold. Two years after his return, Marco Polo was captured during a naval battle and imprisoned. He met the writer Rustichello in prison where he told his stories to him and other fellow prisoners. *The Travels of Marco Polo* was published after his release from prison in 1299.

SCRIPT SUMMARY: MARCO MILLIONS

The narrator introduces this script that is set in a Genoese jail where Marco Polo is being held as a prisoner of war. Another prisoner, Rustichello, is recording stories which Marco is telling other prisoners and a guard about his travels through Asia. Marco Polo describes the journey he took with his father and uncle over mountains and across deserts to the palace of Kublai Khan, ruler of China. He tells of a huge city with over a million people and a Khan who feeds thousands of people at his banquets. Marco recounts stories of many wealthy rulers he encountered on his journey to and from China. He implies that millions of rubies, sapphires, and other gems are in the storehouses of these rulers. Marco tells about gold-covered temples and kings with piles of pearls.

Marco Polo describes many of the unusual cultural practices he encountered, including one where the husband cares for the baby after it is born and the new mother works in the fields. He mentions some things that had not been used in Europe like oil, coal, and paper money. Antonio, a fellow prisoner, Rustichello, and the guard often question the accuracy of some of Marco Polo's statements.

Assignment
Read the readers' theater script "Marco Millions." Prepare for the performances and share your interpretations of the scripts with the class.

Extensions: Geography, Writing, and Literature

- Find a map of Europe and Asia with the travels of Marco Polo recorded. Use textbooks, books about Marco Polo, or Internet sources. Create your own map of his travels. Indicate the modern names for the nations and places he visited.

- Write a script based on one of the events listed below or another one related to the adventures of Marco Polo.

    Meeting Kublai Khan

    Bringing a princess to Persia

    Fighting bandits in the desert

    Dangers on the way to China

    Coming home to Venice

- Read *Marco Polo: To China and Back* by Steven Otfinoski. Use one episode or a chapter as the basis for a readers' theater script about Marco Polo's adventures.

- Read any available version of *The Travels of Marco Polo* by Marco Polo. Use one episode or a chapter as the basis for a readers' theater script about his experiences.

SCRIPT: MARCO MILLIONS

This script is set in a prison where Marco Polo and some of his fellow Venetians have been imprisoned after losing a naval battle with the rival city of Genoa. There are five speaking parts.

Narrator: In the year 1271, 17-year-old Marco Polo left his home in Venice to travel across Asia to China with his father and uncle. The trip took almost four years. It was the elder Polos' second trip to the court of the Mongol emperor, Kublai Khan, who ruled China. Marco Polo kept journals of all his experiences along the journey and his 17-year stay in China, as well as the return voyage. To help time pass in prison, he is recounting his adventures to his guards and fellow prisoners, including a fellow prisoner named Rustichello, who is writing down the stories.

Marco Polo: Let me tell you, friends, Asia is a very different world from Europe. On our journey, we climbed mountains that were thousands of feet high. It took a very long time for food to cook or even to boil water. There was so little air on the huge flat plateau we crossed in the Pamir Mountains that we could barely breathe. The passes between mountains were treacherous and millions of tons of rocks towered over each side.

Antonio: Is Asia all mountains?

Marco Polo: No, we crossed a desert that stretched hundreds of miles.

Rustichello: Was it dangerous?

Marco Polo: It can be dangerous. The caravan we were on was attacked by bandits. Many of our fellow travelers were killed, and all of us lost some of our trade goods. We saw spirits at night who tempted us to wander out onto the desert where you become lost and die. These dream spirits are brought by the heat and burning sun.

Guard: Are the lands rich or poor?

Marco Polo: When we got to the court of the Great Khan in China, we were astounded by the wealth. The walls of his palaces were coated with gold and silver. Thousands of his nobles were dressed in rich fabrics decorated with gold, pearls, and other gems. Near one palace is a giant man-made lake. This palace is surrounded by a city of soldiers and then a larger city of common people. At least a million people live there.

Guard: How could any city support a million people? There wouldn't be enough food or water.

Marco Polo: The people are very productive, and in times of crop loss, the Khan feeds his people from giant storehouses. He can feed millions if necessary.

Antonio: Millions . . . Everything is millions with Marco. Rustichello, you should call your book *Marco Millions*.

Rustichello: What does this Great Khan like to do?

Marco Polo: The Great Khan has banquets where 20,000 people can eat in his banquet hall and 40,000 more outside. The Khan drinks fermented horse milk, and the musicians play their instruments each time he drinks. The emperor goes on hunts with a portable palace, a giant tent carried by elephants and supported by thousands of slaves who set up the tent palace. He has leopards that ride on his horses and leap off to hunt deer in the emperor's forests. Kublai Khan keeps falcons in the top of his tent palace that catch birds in flight.

Rustichello: What other wonders did you see?

Marco Polo: We saw many amazing things on our journey. There was a leak in the earth where black oil poured out of the ground. We saw the natives use this black liquid to keep lamps burning, and they treated their camels and other animals that had skin diseases with this liquid. In another city, people burn black rocks to heat water. They use this hot water for bathing—sometimes as often as three times a week.

Guard: Rocks don't burn.

Antonio: Bathing . . . What a strange custom. I only bathe when it rains or I fall into a canal.

Rustichello: Did you see riches in other kingdoms besides China?

Marco Polo: The leader of one kingdom controls mines in his land where rubies and sapphires are found. There are millions of these bright red gems in the mines, but he is very shrewd. He takes only enough for his own use, and the scarcity of these gems keeps them valuable.

Guard: He always sees millions . . .

Marco Polo: In India, we saw divers go into the sea and bring up beautiful pearls. Millions of these perfect white jewels are found every year. On our journey home, we saw gold worth millions and millions of our coins.

Antonio: More millions!

Rustichello: How do people in China trade for food and clothes?

Marco Polo: In China, the Great Khan has found a way to make trade easy. Carrying enough coins to buy some of the marvels of the Chinese markets would be difficult. Kublai Khan has the inner bark taken from the mulberry tree, the same tree whose leaves are used to feed the insects that produce silk, the richest of all fabrics. This bark is made into a paper, and the paper is cut into different sizes and used for money.

Guard: I suppose there are millions of pieces of this paper money.

Marco Polo: Of course, it is used to buy many things.

Antonio: What were the people like?

Marco Polo: The people of Asia are extraordinarily different. In the land called Mien, we saw a strange practice by peasants. When a mother had her baby, she immediately got out of her bed, and her husband would take her place and care for the child. The mother would do the household chores and work in the fields and come in only to feed the baby.

Guard: That is ridiculous! Surely, Marco, you exaggerate.

Marco Polo: In the capital city of Mien, there were temples built into towers called pagodas. These are covered with gold and silver as thick as your finger. They have gold and silver bells at the top.

Antonio: In Venice, thieves would steal the gold.

Marco Polo: In India, the wife of a man who dies does not choose to live. They burn their dead the same day because of the heat. The wife, no matter how young she is, throws herself on the burning funeral fire. She doesn't want to leave him. It would be improper not to join him in death.

SCRIPT: MARCO MILLIONS (cont.)

Antonio: There's little chance my wife would do that. She'd be out spending my money.

Marco Polo: It is especially sad to see a young teenage wife burned alive with her much older husband. All marriages are arranged, of course, and the wife's family receives a dowry, so some rich old men marry very young women.

Guard: Some rich father should pay me to marry his daughter.

Marco Polo: On one island where we stopped on the way home, the natives wore nothing but cloths tied around their middles. Their king wore only the cloth and a giant necklace covered with rubies, sapphires, emeralds, and pearls. The king of another land owns a ruby as large as your hand and perfectly round and flawless. In other places we saw men who covered their teeth with gold and stained their flesh with pictures of birds and beasts.

Rustichello: Marco, this will make a wonderful book, but it should be fiction. No one will ever believe these stories.

Marco Polo: I have not told the half of what I saw.

Narrator: *The Travels of Marco Polo* was published after his release from prison in 1299. It was an extremely important source for later explorers. Columbus carefully read it. Marco Polo married and lived in Venice until his death in 1324.

READER'S RESPONSE: MARCO MILLIONS

Directions

- These discussion activities and questions may be used in small groups or with the entire class. They may also be used by the actors as a part of their preparation for the reading.
- Refer to the script "Marco Millions" when responding to all questions. You may also find useful facts in the background section, biographies, textbooks, and Internet sources.
- Make notes on the lines provided below each question before your group discussion.

General Discussion

1. What was the most interesting sight or cultural practice that Marco Polo described? Why did it interest you?

_____

_____

2. Why did Marco's friends often make fun of his stories?

_____

_____

3. What place that is as unknown today as Asia was in 1300 would you like to see? Explain your choice.

_____

_____

Making It Personal

Would you like to have traveled with Marco Polo? Why?

_____

_____

_____

Describe what your feelings would be if you were away on a journey for more than 20 years.

_____

_____

_____

Do you think Marco Polo was exaggerating, confused, or telling the exact truth? Explain the reasons for your choice.

_____

_____

_____

Who was the greatest explorer in human history? Give reasons for your choice.

_____

_____

READERS' THEATER

DEATH IN PARIS

BACKGROUND: DEATH IN PARIS

Bubonic Plague

Bubonic plague erupted in the Gobi Desert in the late 1320s and quickly spread to China by 1331 where it killed two-thirds of the entire population over the next twenty years. It then spread westward through India, the Arab lands, and into Europe through the trading cities of Italy in 1347. The epidemic spread almost immediately to Paris and the other cities and villages of France. In less than a year, it swept through England, Scotland, and on to Germany and other northern countries in Europe. It eventually returned to the high plains of Asia where it ended about 1351.

The Black Death

This pandemic quickly became known as the Black Death in Europe where it killed more than one-third of the population and massively changed European life. The disease was carried by ticks that lived on rats and infected them. Rats flourished on all ships and were carried from port to port. The ticks infected sailors, rats living on the wharves, and people who came into contact with them.

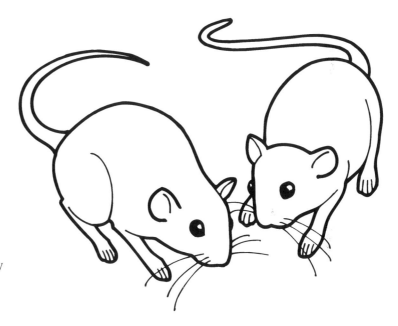

Nobody knew the causes of the plague until modern times, but people did know that the contagion could be spread by contact with those who were infected. They did not realize that the filthy conditions of European cities, the lack of any adequate sanitation, drinking water polluted by human and animal waste, and the fact that people rarely bathed or washed their hands helped spread the contagion.

So many people died that no provisions could be made for the dead. Many doctors, religious leaders, and public officials stayed in cities and tried to help. Others fled to rural areas hoping to avoid the contagion. The depopulation of Europe led to massive shortages of food, labor problems, and to the first cracks in the system of serfdom which had placed most peasants under the absolute control of local landowners and nobles. It took many years for Europe to recover from the plague, and the disease returned several times over the centuries, but not as many people died in these later outbreaks. The disease still exists and people are infected every year in many countries. It can be treated today with antibiotics.

SCRIPT SUMMARY: DEATH IN PARIS

The narrator sets the time and place for this script—Paris, France, 1348. Bubonic plague has spread from Asia into Europe destroying cities and killing millions of people. The scene in this readers' theater is set in the chief magistrate's office with the chief of police, a doctor, and a merchant discussing the situation in Paris that has reached a crisis point.

One out of every three residents of Paris has died from the Black Death. The streets have piles of bodies because so few people are willing or able to remove them. In some houses everyone died. Burial services are forgotten, and some bodies are simply being dumped in trenches. Trade with other cities has virtually ceased. There are shortages of food and labor. Gangs of thugs are roaming the streets and invading homes, and there are not enough police to control them. Doctors have no cure for the contagion. Some people have fled the city hoping to avoid the disease. The poor and the wealthy are equally at risk for death, and the entire structure of civilization seems to be coming down. The narrator concludes the script by citing the causes of the plague, which were ticks living on rats and the unsanitary and crowded living conditions which spread the contagion.

Assignment

Read the readers' theater script "Death in Paris." Prepare for the performances and share your interpretations of the scripts with the class.

Extensions: Writing and Literature

- Write a script based on one of the events listed below or another one related to the Black Death. Use the background section, books about the Black Death, and the Internet as sources of ideas.

    A peasant family is struck by the plague

    A doctor's efforts to save a victim

    A living child surrounded by her family dead from the plague

    Life on ship with the plague killing most of the crew, and nobody willing to let the ship land on shore

- Read *The Black Death* by Phyllis Corzine. Use some of the incidents cited as the basis for a readers' theater script about life during the Black Death.

- Read *A Journal of the Plague Year* by Daniel Defoe, which offers a fictional account of a plague year in London in 1665. Use one episode or a chapter of this fictional but accurate account of life during a plague as the basis for a script.

- Read *Fever 1793* by Laurie Halse Anderson that describes the effects of a Yellow Fever epidemic in Philadelphia. Use a chapter or episode as the basis for a script.

SCRIPT: DEATH IN PARIS

This script describes the horrendous loss of life and the suffering created by the spread of bubonic plague across France in 1348. There are five speaking parts.

Narrator: Bubonic plague rose to epidemic proportions in the Gobi Desert in the late 1320s. This terrible disease would kill two-thirds of the population of China over the next twenty years. It spread across Asia to Constantinople through the Arab lands and entered Europe through the trading cities of Italy. It then spread through France and the rest of Europe in 1348. Towns and cities were unequipped to handle such an epidemic. In this scene, the chief magistrate of Paris, a doctor, the chief of police, and a wealthy merchant are meeting to discuss what to do about the plague.

Magistrate: Gentlemen, what is the situation in Paris right now?

Police Chief: Sir, this great city is in its death throes. The plague has been here for months, and Paris has lost tens of thousands of people. At least one out of every three persons has died, and there is no end in sight. There are so many bodies on the streets that it looks like a city of the dead.

Doctor: The burials no longer have loved ones to mourn for their lost family members. Those who would grieve are dead themselves or fled to the countryside or simply afraid to leave home lest the air bring the plague to them. There are no tears, candles, or lines of mourners to honor the dead. Death is so normal that those being buried are honored as little as if they were simply dead goats.

Merchant: Trade between Paris and other cities has virtually ceased. Everyone knows we have the plague, and no one wants our ships to carry the stench of plague to their ports—although it wouldn't matter. Almost every city and village in all France has it. I have received letters from my business associates all over Europe. The plague is everywhere.

SCRIPT: DEATH IN PARIS (cont.)

Magistrate: Doctor, can nothing be done to halt this Black Death sweeping across our city? Paris has more doctors than any city in Europe and a great hospital.

Doctor: Doctors are dying as fast as the poorest laborers. No medicine works. We have tried bleeding the patients with leeches to remove the bad blood. The patients die anyway. The egg-shaped swellings called buboes that are the sure mark of plague are very hard to drain, and nothing seems to stops the disease. It is difficult even for families to care for the victims.

Magistrate: Religious leaders talk of omens in the heavens and the failure of people to obey the laws of God, but priests, doctors, nursing sisters, people helping the sick, and others known for their piety and kindness are dying as fast as the ungodly. Are any people safe from this plague?

Doctor: No. The Jews have been blamed for poisoning the wells, but they are dying as fast as Christians—and the plague arrived from the sea on ships.

Police Chief: The city has become totally lawless, your honor. People expect to die. Large, rowdy gangs of men and some women are roving the city stealing anything they can from the homes of both the living and the dead. We are helpless to stop the crime. Most of my officers are dead or have fled the city hoping to save their lives. It will do no good. My reports from the farms and villages are very clear. More than half of all the country people have died.

Doctor: Bodies are lying everywhere uncollected. The city workers who are left don't have enough help to remove them. The nuns who have been helping have lost so many sisters to the plague that few are left to do this work. Entire homes are death houses. The animals were dead as well. The plague doesn't spare people or animals.

Magistrate: The cemeteries are full, even the soldiers charged with disposing of them are disappearing—dead by the plague or fled the city.

Merchant: The plague kills without regard for rank or wealth either. Dozens of my wealthy merchant friends are as dead as any poor laborer. Some families have been entirely wiped out. Princess Joan was on the way to marry a king's son. She is dead. The families of nobles are dying as fast as serfs.

Police Chief: The labor shortage is severe too, your honor. There are few men willing to work. Some are afraid to leave their homes, but most are sick or dying. Those who remain want much higher wages and even beatings will not change their minds. The city has almost no reserves of food. Prices are going higher daily for what little food remains.

Magistrate: I have no solution to this problem. I fear that Paris and all France will be nothing but a giant house of death before it ends.

Narrator: The Black Death swept through Europe like a relentless invading army in the years from 1347 to 1351. It killed people in every walk of life and no medical treatment worked. People thought it was carried by the air on ships, but they were unaware that the disease was carried by ticks living on ship rats and that the ticks could infect people and spread the disease. The extremely crowded homes and close living conditions in cities of that time, polluted drinking water, terrible sanitation, and poor personal hygiene all contributed to the spread of the epidemic.

READER'S RESPONSE: DEATH IN PARIS

Directions

- These discussion activities and questions may be used in small groups or with the entire class. They may also be used by the actors as a part of their preparation for the reading.
- Refer to the script "Death in Paris" when responding to all questions. You may also find useful facts in the background section.
- Make notes on the lines provided below each question before your group discussion.

General Discussion

1. What problems face the leaders of Paris?

   _____

   _____

   _____

2. What should the chief magistrate do to help the people of Paris? Explain your answer.

   _____

   _____

   _____

3. What actually caused the plague and what caused it to spread to so many people?

   _____

   _____

   _____

Making It Personal

What would you do if you lived in Paris during the epidemic? Explain your choice.

_____

_____

_____

Describe what your feelings would be if you were caught in the middle of an epidemic like the Black Death.

_____

_____

_____

Do you think there are any situations today where you could be the victim of the plague or any other contagious disease killing many people? Explain your response.

_____

_____

_____

READERS' THEATER

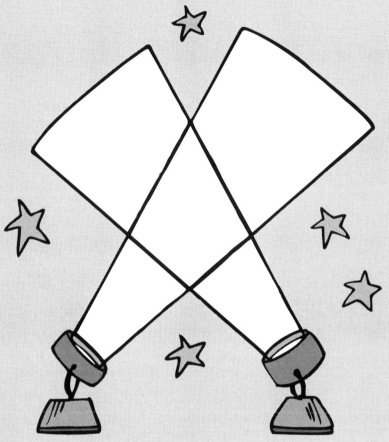

LEONARDO'S STUDIO

BACKGROUND: LEONARDO'S STUDIO

The Italian Renaissance

The Renaissance, the rebirth of learning, art, and science, began in the 1400s in Italy and gradually spread to other European countries. The Italian city-states were like small nations where the wealth of powerful dukes who became rich in trade financed an amazing flowering of painting, sculpture, architecture, and engineering achievements. Renaissance thinkers studied the works of ancient Greek scholars and used them as a basis for new ideas in the arts, mathematics, medicine, and science. The invention of the printing press in 1440 was a powerful agent for spreading learning throughout Europe.

Artists and Thinkers

One of the great artists of the Renaissance was Michelangelo, famed for his sculptures like *David* and his painting on the ceiling of the Sistine chapel. Botticelli, Donatello, Titian, and Raphael were extraordinary artists who influenced the style of art for centuries afterwards. Mathematicians such as Luca Pacioli, astronomers such as Nicolas Copernicus, and political writers such as Niccolo Machiavelli, opened the doors to many modern ideas about man and the universe he inhabits.

Leonardo da Vinci

Leonardo da Vinci was the complete Renaissance man. He was interested in every aspect of life. His painting and sculpture demonstrated new concepts of harmony, proportion, and style. Da Vinci had a fascination with human and animal anatomy. He sought to find mathematical perfection in human design and correct proportion in all forms of life. He had very modern ideas about sanitation for cities and was considered finicky about cleanliness, even though he was also willing to cut through rotting flesh to dissect the corpses of dead people.

Leonardo da Vinci

Leonardo studied the principles of flight, the movement of water, the behavior of air currents, the nature of geometry, and a host of other scientific topics. He kept journals and papers of all of his studies written left-handed and in mirror writing. He was disorganized, easily irritated, and vain about his looks and his intellect. Leonardo tended to leave many paintings and projects unfinished, including the *Mona Lisa*. Most of his designs could not be turned into working models because the technology did not yet exist to create models.

SCRIPT SUMMARY: LEONARDO'S STUDIO

The action takes place in the studio of Leonardo da Vinci, a brilliant artist, scientist, and engineer of the Italian Renaissance. The speakers include the following: the Duchess, who is the model for the *Mona Lisa*; Luca, a mathematician friend; Ludovico, the Duke of Milan and Leonardo's patron; and Salai, Leonardo's sassy apprentice and adoptive son.

The Duchess would like to get her portrait finished. An underlying theme of the script is Leonardo's tendency to leave work unfinished. Ludovico praises Leonardo for the Masque of the Planets, a giant, moving diorama-like mini-drama he did for a wedding and for his clay model of a horse that the duke would like cast in bronze.

All of the characters become involved in the various designs on display in the workshop. They examine Leonardo's plans for flying machines and a parachute and his sketches of birds. They are especially intrigued by Leonardo's anatomical drawings of the human body done by dissecting the corpses of poor people. The duke is especially impressed by Leonardo's designs for weapons: a bow that fires many arrows, a catapult, and a cannon. The narrator concludes the script with a review of Leonardo's multiple accomplishments and talents.

Assignment

Read the readers' theater script "Leonardo's Studio." Prepare for the performances and share your interpretations of the scripts with the class.

Extensions: Writing and Literature

- Write a script based on one of the events listed below or another one related to the Renaissance or the life of Leonardo da Vinci. Use the background section, biographies of Leonardo and other Renaissance artists, and books about the Renaissance for ideas and topics for your script.

   A scene from Leonardo's early apprenticeship to the painter Verrocchio

   Leonardo's artistic battle with Michelangelo

   Life in an Italian city-state in the late 1400s

   Leonardo's discussions with the woman who modeled for the *Mona Lisa*

   Leonardo's relationship with his apprentice and adoptive son, Salai

- Read *Leonardo da Vinci: Genius of Art and Science* by Jennifer Reed. Use one episode or a chapter as the basis for a readers' theater script about Leonardo's life.

- Read *The Second Mrs. Gioconda* by E. L. Konigsburg. Use one episode or a chapter of this novel as the basis for a readers' theater script about Leonardo and his companions.

SCRIPT: LEONARDO'S STUDIO

This script introduces some people in the life of Leonardo da Vinci and illustrates the extraordinary range of interests of this man who is the model for the term "Renaissance Man," a person of multiple talents and monumental energy. The characters include Leonardo, Ludovico (Duke of Milan), a Duchess, Salai (a young, sassy apprentice), and Luca, a friend. There are six speakers.

Narrator: The scene takes place at Leonardo da Vinci's studio in Milan, Italy, in the late 1400s. Famous for his paintings and other interests, the middle-aged Leonardo is often employed by the city's ruler, Duke Ludovico Sforza, as engineer, architect, painter, and designer of masques (short dramatic scenes with great imagery).

Duchess: Leonardo, my friend, when will my portrait be finished? No other artist takes years to complete a portrait.

Salai: You expect it finished? What a strange idea. There are paintings all over Italy, Duchess, that the great Leonardo has started but not completed. Possibly, you should ask Michelangelo to complete it. He finishes his projects. Of course, he is said to be just as difficult to satisfy as our Leonardo.

Luca: Salai, you are hopelessly disrespectful.

Ludovico: Leonardo, you are a genius. The horse you sculpted out of clay is a magnificent giant. It must be 20 feet high. The proportions are perfect. It will be magnificent when it is molded in bronze. It will be the greatest sculpture in all Italy. Even Michelangelo will be envious.

Salai: If it ever gets done. Of course, you and Michelangelo could work on it together. You get along so well.

SCRIPT: LEONARDO'S STUDIO (cont.)

Duchess: Don't be fresh, Salai. Everyone knows that Michelangelo is a hot-tempered genius. He drives his patrons crazy. No one would expect two such proud geniuses to be friends.

Ludovico: The Masque of the Planets was very dramatic, Leonardo. We must do another such scene to highlight your skills as an engineer. The sight of those planets and stars revolving on the stage amazed all of my guests. It was the highlight of my nephew's marriage feast. It was the talk of Milan for months.

Duchess: It was truly magnificent, Leonardo. What are these drawings? The birds are beautiful. You have them actually flying across the paper. I love the kites, too.

Leonardo: These are designs for flying machines, Duchess. Sometime men will fly. These machines would be the vehicles for flight.

Ludovico: And what are these contraptions with a man hanging in them?

Leonardo: They will help men fall from the sky without crashing. The parachute will slow the fall so that a man will land as soft as a feather.

Salai: Of course, when men fly by flapping their arms in these winged machines, they will want to jump out of the air and float to the earth. My master is a great dreamer.

Luca: Be silent, Salai. Study these geometric figures, sir. Look at the drawings. The figures are hollow. You can actually see through the cube and the octahedron. I am a mathematician, and I have never seen such drawings.

Ludovico: These human drawings are magnificent, Leonardo. They are absolutely real. Every feature of the arms and legs, skin and bones is perfect.

Duchess: Is this what we look like inside our bodies, Leonardo? It is fortunate we are covered by skin, or no one could stand to look at each other. They are disgusting, but I can't tear my eyes away from them.

Ludovico: The bones are each shaped in such different ways.

Leonardo: My dear patron, the skeleton works like a system of levers. The muscles allow them to move in very specific directions.

Ludovico: Leonardo, you say that you dissect corpses to study the human body for your magnificent drawings. Where are the bodies?

Leonardo: Well, I do my dissections at the hospitals. In 30 years, I have dissected 30 male and female corpses of different ages. I dissect the poor, executed criminals, and the aged. It is seldom that I get a dead person who has a healthy body.

Salai: It is so amazing how you can tolerate doing such a thing!

SCRIPT: LEONARDO'S STUDIO (cont.)

Ludovico: I love these building plans. You are a great architect, Leonardo. We must build some of these magnificent structures in the future. This looks like a design for the entire city.

Leonardo: It is designed to keep the plague from killing thousands of our people as it did years ago. This city will be clean and open. Filth of all kinds will be carried away from where people live.

Salai: Your honor, possibly you should build this ship, too. It is designed to sail underwater and attack enemy ships.

Leonardo: I have not finished all of the details yet.

Ludovico: This giant bow will fire many arrows at one time. What an idea! Can we build one? These cannons are magnificent. They are clearly more powerful than anything we have to protect our city. So is this catapult that would smash a wall in one or two launches. We must build these weapons.

Leonardo: That is the intention, my patron. Of course, some of the materials do not yet exist to build them.

Duchess: What are these instruments?

Leonardo: The first is a clock that wakens me, so I do not waste the early morning. The instruments are my models for improved string instruments and a sweeter-sounding horn.

Ludovico: What is this sculpture?

Leonardo: It moves, your honor, or it will. The legs of the lion will move with a mechanical crank.

Salai: Of course, it is unfinished . . . but can you imagine the reactions of someone meeting an iron lion?

Luca: You have an amazing mind, my friend Leonardo. Even if you never finish your projects, the ideas will help future thinkers. I am glad that you have kept so many journals and papers, so others can see your ideas.

Salai: If they can ever read his notes, written left-handed and backwards.

Duchess: At least it makes the many trips here worthwhile, although I truly wish you would finish my portrait.

Leonardo: It must be as perfect as your own face, my Mona Lisa.

Narrator: Leonardo da Vinci designed many ideas that did become real inventions in the future. He sketched simple planes, helicopters, parachutes, tanks, machine guns, sewing machines, hand tools, submarines, musical instruments, and many different machines. He anticipated discoveries in disease prevention, astronomy, and the laws of motion. He was a brilliant painter, sculptor, architect, and engineer. Leonardo was a true Renaissance man.

READER'S RESPONSE: LEONARDO'S STUDIO

Directions

- These discussion activities and questions may be used in small groups or with the entire class. They may also be used by the actors as a part of their preparation for the reading.
- Refer to the script "Leonardo's Studio" when responding to all questions. You may also find useful facts in the background section, in biographies of Leonardo da Vinci, and Internet sites.
- Make notes on the lines provided below each question before your group discussion.

General Discussion

1. Why do you think Leonardo dissected human bodies even though he was not a doctor?

_____

_____

_____

2. What designs, inventions, or sculpture most impressed Ludovico? Why did these appeal to him?

_____

_____

_____

3. Who do you think most appreciated Leonardo as a person and an artist? Explain your choice.

_____

_____

_____

4. In your opinion, what was Leonardo's greatest strength as a person, and what was his greatest weakness?

_____

_____

_____

Making It Personal

What question would you most want to ask Leonardo? Why?

_____

_____

_____

_____

Would you like to be like Leonardo? Explain your answer.

_____

_____

_____

_____

Which of Leonardo's inventions and designs are closest to modern inventions? Explain your answer.

_____

_____

_____

_____

READERS' THEATER

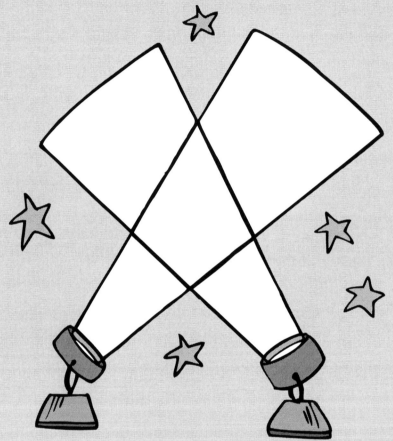

FORTUNE FAVORS THE BOLD

32

BACKGROUND: FORTUNE FAVORS THE BOLD

The Conquistadores

The discovery of the New World by Christopher Columbus led to a major effort by the Spanish government to find gold and other forms of wealth in the new lands. The Spanish settlement in Cuba became a staging ground for exploration of the Yucatan Peninsula. Many of the soldiers who made up these expeditions were adventurers from Spain like Hernando Cortés to whom the New World offered opportunities for wealth and adventure.

Hernando Cortés

Hernando Cortés was sent to study law by his parents, but he tired of that study and decided to travel to the new world. A friend in Hispaniola helped him get an estate worked by Indian slaves. Cortés became involved in several expeditions and a half-hearted marriage. Cortés quickly became wealthy and got the approval of Governor Valasquez to finance his own expedition to the Yucatan Peninsula to discover new lands in an area that rumor said was filled with gold.

The Conquest

Cortés became immediately involved in conflict with local natives after he landed in the area he called Vera Cruz. He quickly demonstrated his shrewd military ability by defeating a much larger force of Tabascans. He found that the natives had never seen either horses or cannons and that they believed both might be gods. In the peace negotiations, Cortés was given a slave named Malinche who spoke both Mayan and Aztec. He was thus able to communicate with the Aztec ambassadors who monitored his travels across Mexico. Malinche helped explain the cultural beliefs of the Aztecs and other tribes he encountered, including the Aztec belief that a white god would return to Mexico and destroy them in the very year of Cortés arrival. She also bore him a son.

Hernando Cortés

Montezuma, the Aztec king, tried to buy Cortés off with gifts of gold and treasure; but the gifts only made him greedy. Cortés made alliances with other tribes who were angry at the Aztecs for their taxes, which included many young people to sacrifice to their gods. Cortés and his men entered Tenochtitlan, the Aztec capital, as the unwelcome guests of Montezuma. The Aztecs later drove the Spanish from the city. Cortés combined his army with native troops and destroyed the capital in a three-month siege in 1521. The wealth of this Aztec empire made Spain and Cortés very rich.

SCRIPT SUMMARY: FORTUNE FAVORS THE BOLD

The setting for this story is the estate of Hernando Cortés in Mexico where Malinche lives. Three of the soldiers who fought alongside Cortés have dropped by in hopes of seeing him again. The four friends discuss the events that led to the conquest of the Aztec empire. They discuss Cortés' amusing early adventures and conflicts with Governor Velasquez. The soldiers and Malinche describe the first major battle against the Tabascans where Cortés shrewdly played on native misconceptions about horses and cannons.

Malinche describes her role as a translator of languages and interpreter of the beliefs of native tribes and the Aztecs. She tells how she was given to Cortés as a part of a peace agreement. The men describe the bold action of Cortés in burning his ships in the harbor of Vera Cruz so that his soldiers knew they had no choice but to go forward with him. They discuss Aztec human sacrifices and other cultural differences between the Spanish and the natives. The soldiers describe their visit to Tenochtitlan and their bitter battle to escape from the Aztecs there. The men discuss the destruction of that city by the Spanish soldiers and their native allies. The narrator concludes with a discussion of the human cost of the conflict.

Assignment

Read the readers' theater script "Fortune Favors the Bold." Prepare for the performances and share your interpretations of the scripts with the class.

Extensions: Writing and Literature

- Write a script based on one of these events or another one related to the era of the conquistadores. Use the background section, textbooks, biographies, and the Internet for help.

  Life as a soldier in Cortés' army

  A scene describing part of Malinche's life as a slave before she met Cortés or as his companion after they met

  Life in Tenochtitlan before the Spanish arrival

  The siege of Tenochtitlan and its fall

  Life as an Aztec farmer or tradesman

- Read *The Feathered Serpent* by Scott O'Dell. Use one episode or a chapter as the basis for a readers' theater script about the interactions of Spanish soldiers with Mayans and Aztecs in the conquest of Mexico.

- Read a biography of Hernando Cortés, Cabeza de Vaca, or Francisco Pizarro. Use one episode or a chapter of this biography as the basis for a readers' theater script.

SCRIPT: FORTUNE FAVORS THE BOLD

This script describes the conquest of the Aztec empire in Mexico by Hernando Cortés from the perspective of several of the participants. There are five speakers.

Narrator: Three of the Spanish conquistadores who fought alongside Hernando Cortés in the conquest of the Aztec civilization in Mexico have gathered at his estate to talk over old times with Malinche, the Indian translator who used her knowledge of the Aztec language and other native languages and cultures to help Cortés achieve his victory.

Diego: I hear the captain-general is in Spain entertaining His Majesty King Charles with his heroic exploits and presenting him with ships filled with gold and jewels. I had hoped to see our leader again.

Malinche: He will return eventually. He hopes to become governor-general of Mexico, but I do not think it will happen. I suspect the Spanish king will not trust any man as determined as Hernando to control his empire.

Porfirio: It was an exciting time, was it not? Remember when Cortés had to hide from Governor Velasquez in a church, and he was finally arrested. If our leader had not bribed his guards to set him free, he might still be there.

Diego: It is remarkable that Velasquez ever let him lead the expedition to the Yucatan Peninsula. He didn't trust our general, but Cortés did spend his own money to outfit the expedition and recruited the 500 soldiers of fortune like ourselves who went with him.

Malinche: The Tabascans, who had bought me as a slave from my own mother, had no chance against Hernando. They outnumbered you conquistadores more than 100 to 1, but their weapons could not pierce the Spanish armor, and your weapons were terribly fearsome. They had never heard cannon before. The cannons seemed like living monsters that spat out fire and death.

Diego: Our swords cut through their cloth armor like a knife through butter. We killed the Tabascans by the hundreds, but we would have eventually been overwhelmed if General Cortés had not brought the horses from the ship.

Malinche: None of the Tabascans had even seen horses. They thought the man and horse was one god that could split in two. The horses were very fast, and the horse soldiers terrified the native warriors.

Porfirio: I was one of those riders. We rode through the Indian lines, and they fled in terror. Captives told me later they expected to be eaten by these god-horses.

Malinche: Captain-general Cortés was very shrewd in his understanding of Indian fears.

Bernal: True. After the fight with the Tabascans, when he agreed to meet and make peace, he had a cannon filled with a powerful load of gunpowder and shot. We fired it, but the Tabascans thought it must be a living creature exploding with fury.

Diego: Then the captain brought out his giant stallion and had it rear and roar and stomp the ground. He told the leaders that the horse was angry at his kindness in making peace.

Malinche: I was part of those terms of peace. I was a slave along with 20 other women given to the captain as a peace offering. The captain quickly learned that I spoke both Aztec and Mayan. I became his special advisor and his girlfriend. I helped him not only translate the native languages, but I also helped him understand how the Aztecs and other peoples thought.

Bernal: Captain Cortés knew that some of our comrades were still loyal to Governor Velasquez and intended to mutiny and return to our home base in Cuba. He seemed to sense when the men were rebellious.

Diego: That's why he ordered his most loyal followers like us to burn our ships so that the men had no choice but to follow him to Mexico. A lot of the men were tired of fighting and were anxious to return home.

Porfirio: But he cleverly left one ship that he said anyone wanting to return to Cuba could use. He asked for those who wanted to return to step forward. Some men did and he knew they could not be trusted because they were loyal to Governor Valasquez. He had us burn the last ship after all and sentenced two rebels to death. Several other malcontents were whipped. He is one tough and dangerous man, our captain general.

Malinche: The other tribes who feared the Aztecs soon learned that, too. Remember how he shrewdly forced the Cholulans and Tlaxcalans to join our side. He made it look to the Aztecs as if they had already joined us. Of course, they soon became willing allies anyway, because they hated having to provide so many young people to be used in human sacrifice on Aztec altars.

Malinche: Our captain was very clever in convincing Montezuma, the Aztec leader, to provide many gifts and allow us into his city.

Diego: But, we were almost destroyed by the Aztecs in our Noche Triste (Sad Night). We retreated from the capital city with the Aztecs severely beating us. We lost half of our Spanish warriors and thousands of native allies. Cortés himself was wounded in the leg and had a fractured skull. We were lucky to escape with our lives.

Porfirio: Remember the Spanish saying, "Fortune Always Favors the Bold."

Diego: Our Captain-general was very bold. He was not willing to return to Cuba, even though the governor sent soldiers to bring him back. He talked those soldiers into joining us. He convinced the tribes who hated the Aztecs for their human sacrifices and their heavy taxes to join us. Those months of battle when we finally captured Tenochtitlan were terrible.

Porfirio: It was a great victory, but it was terrible to see such a great city destroyed.

Narrator: The final siege of Tenochtitlan lasted from April till August 13, 1521, when the city was finally captured. At least a quarter of a million Aztecs were killed or died of starvation and disease along with 30,000 native allies. Hernando Cortés was eventually appointed captain-general of New Spain. He ran into trouble with those who distrusted him and eventually returned to Spain where he was unable to convince King Charles to allow him complete authority as governor. He died in Spain largely forgotten and ignored.

READER'S RESPONSE: FORTUNE FAVORS THE BOLD

Directions

- These discussion activities and questions may be used in small groups or with the entire class. They may also be used by the actors as a part of their preparation for the reading.
- Refer to the script "Fortune Favors the Bold" when responding to all questions. You may also find useful facts in the background section, textbooks, biographies, and the Internet.
- Make notes on the lines provided below each question before your group discussion.

General Discussion

1. What were the good effects of the conquest of the Aztecs? Explain your answer.

_____

_____

_____

2. What were the bad effects of the conquest of the Aztecs? Explain your answer.

_____

_____

_____

3. What might have happened to the Aztecs if Cortés had not conquered them? Offer several suggestions.

_____

_____

_____

Making It Personal

With whom do you sympathize—Cortés and his soldiers or the Aztecs? Explain your choice.

_____

_____

_____

How would you feel if you were Malinche, the slave girl given to Cortés who became his translator and advisor?

_____

_____

_____

How do you feel about Cortés? Was he a hero or a villain? Explain your answer.

_____

_____

READERS' THEATER

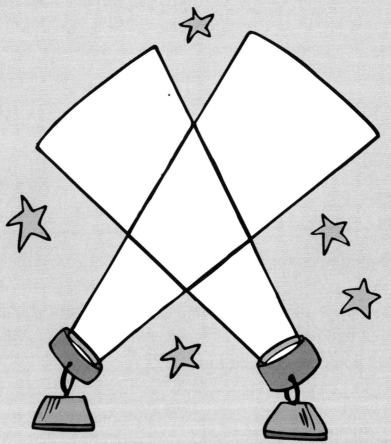

SHE'S THE BOSS

BACKGROUND: SHE'S THE BOSS

Elizabeth I and the Elizabethan Age

Elizabeth I is considered by many to be the most successful and powerful monarch in British history. She came to the throne at the age of 25, the last living child of Henry VIII. She had been a brilliant student. Elizabeth was proficient in French, Italian, Spanish, and Flemish, among the modern languages, and mastered the ancient languages of Greek and Latin. She learned history, mathematics, geography, astronomy, and even studied architecture.

Her father spent most of his life trying to find a wife who would bear him a strong son to inherit the British throne. He never realized that, of his three children, Elizabeth was the strongest in both will and physical energy. Her mother was beheaded at her father's order when she was only two years old. Nonetheless, Elizabeth developed as a perceptive and practical child.

Her brother, Edward, died young and her sister, Mary, died after nearly five years as queen. Elizabeth took the throne as England was suffering from a great deal of religious conflict between Catholics and Protestants. The country had huge debts and had suffered heavy losses in a war with France.

Elizabeth

Elizabeth secretly supported the piracy of John Hawkins and Francis Drake who robbed Spanish ships and sent a portion of the stolen gold to her. She eventually knighted Sir Francis Drake and gave him command of the English fleet. Drake defeated the Spanish Armada in 1588 in one the most important naval battles in history. The victory made England one of the great powers in the world.

Elizabeth flirted with marriage to several kings of Europe and English dukes, but it was clear to most advisors that she really had no intention of having her power compromised by any male. She was in charge of England, and she never lost track of her intention to rule. She very reluctantly executed her cousin Mary, Queen of Scots, because Mary had conspired against her.

Creative arts, especially drama and writing, flourished in England under her reign. She favored William Shakespeare and other British writers with her support. Elizabeth was generally admired and loved by most of her subjects who called her "Good Queen Bess," a name that suggested a gentler and softer person than she ever was.

SCRIPT SUMMARY: SHE'S THE BOSS

This script is set in one of Elizabeth I's palaces in London in the later years of Elizabeth's long reign as Queen of England. The leaders of England are in attendance. The speakers include the explorer, pirate, and admiral, Sir Francis Drake, and the adventurer, Sir Walter Raleigh. William Shakespeare is in attendance and *Romeo and Juliet* had been performed for the guests before the script opens. A countess and duchess provide gossip about the guests.

Sir Walter Raleigh tells Elizabeth of his intention of naming the first English colony in the New World, Virginia, in her honor. Elizabeth was called "the Virgin Queen" because she was unmarried. Sir Francis Drake also dances with the queen and describes his heroic and successful exploits in robbing the Spanish galleons and defeating the Spanish Armada.

William Shakespeare dances with Elizabeth and discusses *Romeo and Juliet*. He tells Elizabeth that she would have been a wonderful Juliet, if women had been allowed to act on the stage. All roles were played by men in that era. The Countess and Duchess offer critical comments about the efforts of the great men of England to flatter the queen and her fondness for the attention. They also indicate that she never surrenders control of the kingdom to any man. She's the boss and everyone knows it.

Assignment

Read the readers' theater script "She's the Boss." Prepare for the performances and share your interpretations of the scripts with the class.

Extensions: Writing and Literature

- Write a script based on one of the events listed below or another one related to the Elizabethan Age. Use the background section, biographies, textbooks, and Internet sources for details and ideas.

  Life in Elizabeth's court

  The defeat of the Spanish Armada

  A scene based on a Shakespearean play

  Sir Walter Raleigh lays his cloak on the ground for the queen

  Drake's trip around the world

  Drake attacks a Spanish fleet of ships carrying gold to Spain

- Read *Beware, Princess Elizabeth* by Carolyn Meyer. Use one episode or a chapter as the basis for a readers' theater script about life before Elizabeth becomes queen.

- Read *Elizabeth I: Red Rose of the House of Tudor* by Kathryn Lasky. Use one episode or a chapter of this fictional diary as the basis for a readers' theater script about Elizabeth when she was eleven years old.

SCRIPT: SHE'S THE BOSS

This script offers a glimpse of Elizabethan life and the people who brought England to power in the 1500s. There are seven speakers.

Narrator: The scene opens at a very fancy London party hosted at Queen Elizabeth I's castle. The early evening entertainment features a play by William Shakespeare performed at her court. The most powerful men in England are in attendance. Among the courtiers are such powerful and famous men as Sir Francis Drake, William Shakespeare, and Sir Walter Raleigh, all of whom owe their wealth and power to Elizabeth's favor.

Sir Walter Raleigh: *(Greeting the Queen and kissing her hand)* Your Majesty, you are a breath of spring. Your beauty radiates across this room and across England like a spring breeze bringing youth and vitality to the nation you so nobly lead. Would you honor me with the first dance?

Elizabeth: Oh, Sir Walter, you are such a flatterer. Yes, do let us dance. I just love drifting across the floor on your arm.

Countess: *(Whispering to a Duchess)* Did you ever hear such a bunch of blather in your life! I swear, Sir Walter Raleigh could flatter the warts off an old toad. Did you see him last winter spreading his magnificent red cloak over the yard, so Her Majesty wouldn't get her royal feet muddy? It was disgusting—even if it was very courtly. I'm surprised he didn't pick her up and carry her.

Duchess: *(Whispering)* She can certainly lap up the flattery like a kitten after spilled milk. Elizabeth is well past the days when she was a young queen courted by the great kings of Europe. She wears a wig, you know. She's totally bald under that bright red hair. I saw for myself when her maids were helping her get ready for the party.

Sir Walter Raleigh: You know that the colony I am sponsoring in the New World has been named Virginia in your honor as our Virgin Queen. After all, no man is worthy of you.

Sir Francis Drake: Your Majesty, may I have the honor of the next dance? As your great sea warrior, I will feel cheated if I should miss the opportunity.

Elizabeth: But, of course, my admiral. Tell me again, Sir Francis, about some of your adventures. I especially enjoy how you stole entire shiploads of gold from our Spanish adversaries. King Philip was very vexed with me over your privateering.

Sir Francis Drake: It was your support that was so important, Your Majesty. I was able to outfit our ships with the best weapons and the finest pirates (privateers, if you prefer). We used brilliant maneuvers to attack those slow-moving Spanish galleons as they headed back to Spain from the New World with their holds filled with gold. We were always outnumbered, but we seldom lost a ship. It was a pleasure to share the gold with you. My circumnavigation of the globe also gave me the opportunity to claim many lands in your name.

Countess:
You notice, Sir Francis didn't mention being chased by several Spanish ships and that the only way he could get home was by going around the world through the Pacific Ocean.

Elizabeth:
King Phillip did get very angry when I held the sword on your shoulder and made you a knight of the realm. Tell us about your defeat of his Spanish Armada.

Sir Francis Drake:
The Spaniards are not as skilled as we English in seafaring, Your Highness. He left his huge assembly of ships all bottled up in port, and we set several old ships on fire and sailed them directly into his fleet. His ships caught on fire and the Almighty Himself assisted us. A wind rose and spread the fires from ship to ship. We sailed into battle with the wind on our side, and our longer guns and faster ships simply shattered his clumsy ships. The remaining vessels were destroyed trying to escape in windy seas.

Countess:
Sir Francis boasts about as well as Sir Walter can flatter, even if it was the greatest naval victory in history.

William Shakespeare:
Your Majesty, did you enjoy the performance of *Romeo and Juliet* this evening?

Elizabeth:
It was magnificent, Mr. Shakespeare. I cried and cheered and felt like I was a part of the performance. It is a pity that women can't take parts on the stage. Using only men must be a challenge.

William Shakespeare: Indeed, Your Majesty, perhaps at some time in the future, the stage will be open to females, too. You would have played a marvelous Juliet.

Countess: Another flatterer. Of course, it should be easy for a playwright.

Duchess: Well, I admire Elizabeth. She has made England one of the great powers of the world, and she succeeded because she controlled men so well. She still pretends that she's available for marriage, even at her age. But I don't think she ever intended to marry. She's never going to let a man or any other woman either control her or England. She's in charge, period. She even had her cousin, Mary, Queen of Scots beheaded for opposing her.

Countess: I agree. She enjoys flattery and lets men boast, but she is the boss; and all of these men here know it, even if they don't like it. After all, what would you expect. Her father had her own mother beheaded when Elizabeth was only two.

Narrator: Elizabeth I became queen at the age of 25 and ruled England for 45 years. It became the strongest naval power in the world and a nation known for its outstanding writers and thinkers. She was known to her subjects by the gentle name "Good Queen Bess." Her enemies found that she was a much tougher, more determined, and intelligent person than her image to the public suggested.

READER'S RESPONSE: SHE'S THE BOSS

Directions

- These discussion activities and questions may be used in small groups or with the entire class. They may also be used by the actors as a part of their preparation for the reading.
- Refer to the script of "She's the Boss" when responding to all questions. You may also find useful facts in the background section, biographies, textbooks, and Internet sources.
- Make notes on the lines provided below each question before your group discussion.

General Discussion

1. Which of the men in the story was most important to Elizabeth? Explain your choice.

_____

_____

_____

2. Why do you think Elizabeth didn't get married? Do you think it was a good decision? Explain your answer.

_____

_____

_____

3. Are women sufficiently strong and capable to run a country? Give three reasons for your answer.

_____

_____

_____

_____

Making It Personal

Which of the men at court did you admire the most? Explain your choice.

_____

_____

_____

Describe what your feelings would be if you were a queen in charge of a country as Elizabeth was. What would you want to do? Of whom or what would you be afraid?

_____

_____

_____

Would you prefer to live in a country under a ruler like a king or queen or in a country where the leaders are elected? Explain your choice.

_____

_____

_____

READERS' THEATER

NEWTON'S APPLE

48

BACKGROUND: NEWTON'S APPLE

Natural Philosophers

An English poet wrote: "Nature and nature's laws lay hid in night: God said, 'Let Newton be!' And all was light!" It was not that simple, but Isaac Newton added immeasurably to the new scientific ideas in physics, astronomy, math, and other sciences which had sprung from the works of Galileo Galilei, Nicolas Copernicus, René Descartes, and other natural philosophers, the name given to scientists in the Age of Reason. These ideas about planets, physical laws, light, and many other features of the natural world would provide the scientific basis for the many inventions and discoveries of the Enlightenment Age in the 1700s.

Isaac Newton

Isaac Newton was born on Christmas Day in 1642 after his father's death. His mother soon married a wealthy neighbor, but left Isaac in the care of his grandparents. He grew up feeling rejected and unloved. Isaac became a good student at the local grammar school mostly to spite a bully who picked on him. In his youth, Newton made many ingenious devices and toys. He was fascinated by the chemicals used by the druggist with whom he lived. He did make friends with the druggist's daughter, Catherine. His mother soon decided Isaac would make a poor farmer, and he went to Cambridge University at his uncle's suggestion.

Newton was a friendless student who paid for part of his expenses by serving wealthier students. He did demonstrate remarkable skill in mathematics. His greatest discoveries were made at home during the plague years when he worked out the universal law of gravitation and the inverse square law expressing the force of gravitation. He also codified the three laws of motion and did remarkable experiments with light. He worked out the principles of calculus that he called "fluxions."

Isaac Newton

Newton returned to Cambridge and was made a mathematics professor at the age of 26. He always had problems making and keeping friends and often quarreled with other scientists over credit for discoveries. He wrote one of the greatest science books ever written, *Mathematical Principles of Natural Philosophy*, in the 1680s. He did further studies in astronomy, wrote a book on light, invented the reflecting telescope, and tried to convert cheap metals into gold. Newton never married. He died at the age of 84 in 1727.

SCRIPT SUMMARY: NEWTON'S APPLE

The setting for this script is an English manor (large farm) during the years 1665 and 1666 when Isaac Newton has returned home to avoid the plague in London. It is a summer evening and three acquaintances—Catherine, John, and Edward—have come to visit. An apple falling from a tree grabs Isaac's attention, and he explains with great enthusiasm to the others how gravity works both on Earth and between the moon and Earth. He describes his discovery of the inverse square law. For example, if the moon were moved twice the distance from Earth, the gravitation pull would be only one-fourth as great.

Newton describes the laws of motion that he has been studying and how they affect things as simple as a moving apple or a ball hit by a stick. His discussion of light and his experiments with prisms interest and amuse his visitors. His visitors remind Isaac of some of his boyhood inventions, including a mouse-driven mill and burning kites flying in the night.

Edward is clearly the most interested in the science Isaac is trying to explain. John thinks he's somewhat odd, and Catherine wishes Isaac would pay more attention to her and a possible future as a simple farmer. The narrator concludes with some basic facts about Newton's career.

Assignment

Read the readers' theater script "Newton's Apple." Prepare for the performances and share your interpretations of the scripts with the class.

Extensions: Writing and Literature

- Write a script based on one of the events listed below or another one related to Isaac Newton, Galileo, Descartes, or other scientists of the time. Use the background section, biographies, textbooks, and Internet sources for help.

   Newton's arguments with Robert Hooke or Gottfried von Leibniz over his discoveries

   Newton's relationship with his young niece, Catherine Barton

   Newton's work as warden of the mint

   Queen Anne makes Newton a British knight.

   A scene from Newton's childhood dealing with his mother, his small inventions, his school days, or his fight with the bully

- Read *Isaac Newton* by Kathleen Krull. Use one episode or a chapter as the basis for a readers' theater script about a facet of Isaac Newton's life. After practicing your script, share your performance with the rest of the class.

SCRIPT: NEWTON'S APPLE

This script is set in a small English manor, a farm where Isaac Newton is doing some of the most extraordinary science investigations ever done in one place by one person. There are five speakers.

Narrator: Twenty-two-year-old Isaac Newton has been sent home from Cambridge University in London, England, in the summer of 1665 because the bubonic plague has hit the city. As many people as possible, including all college students, have been sent away to reduce the number of potential deaths. Newton is sitting under an apple tree in the evening with a girl and two village acquaintances. An apple falls from the tree. He picks up the apple and looks at it and then at the moon.

Isaac: An apple falls. It doesn't go back up. It always falls straight down toward Earth—toward the center of Earth. It doesn't fly off into space. It falls straight down.

John: Did you think it should fall up—not down? Is that what you learned in your fancy college, Newton? You could have stayed right here at your mother's manor and figured that out.

Catherine: Isaac, I don't know what you see in that college, anyway. I missed you here.

Isaac: You see, Catherine, the apple is attracted to Earth. The rocks are attracted to Earth. Even the softest dirt and the lightest flower seed are attracted to Earth. If they weren't attracted, they would just float off into space. Even the moon is attracted to Earth. All of the heavenly bodies are attracted to Earth. Everything is attracted to Earth.

Edward: Yes, and the heavier we are, the more attracted we are. See, I'm a lot more attracted than you skinny people.

Isaac: You're right, Edward. The greater the weight and the shorter the distance between the two objects, the greater the attraction.

Catherine: Isaac, haven't you forgotten something else that is attractive?

Isaac: No, Catherine, everything is attracted to Earth, and Earth is attracted to everything else. Earth is attracted to the moon. Earth is attracted to the stars. Earth is attracted to the sun. Earth is attracted to everything else. The closer the distance between the heavenly bodies and Earth, the greater the attraction.

Catherine: I'm very attracted to you, Isaac.

Isaac: Of course, Catherine. It's gravity, you see. It works everywhere in the heavens, on Earth, and throughout the cosmos.

John: I'm not sure this college boy is nearly as smart as he's supposed to be.

Edward: Can you measure this gravity, like water or string?

Isaac: Yes, I have spent weeks working out the equations. My workbooks are filled with the numbers. I have determined that an inverse square law governs this attraction. The farther one object is from another, the less the attraction. If the moon moved twice as far from Earth, the attraction would only be one-fourth as great. If it moved three times as far away, the force of gravity would only be one-ninth as strong.

SCRIPT: NEWTON'S APPLE (cont.)

Edward: Well, if anyone moves the moon, we're in trouble, I guess, because by that figuring, it might drift off into space.

Isaac: Indeed, it would be less attracted to Earth.

Catherine: But Isaac, if the moon vanished, what would lovers do? There'd be no moonlight for kissing!

Isaac: But Catherine, the same calculations could be used to send objects into space. Using my system, which I call fluxions, an engineer could design cannons that shoot balls into space. Giant catapults could launch huge arrows into the heavens.

John: Isaac, you spend too much time dreaming. Nobody is going to fire cannons at the moon or arrows into the heavens.

Catherine: You have a very nice farm here. You could become a successful farmer if you gave up all of this fancy daydreaming.

Edward: Of course, you would have to remember to keep the pigs in their pen and the cows in the pasture, so they don't go wandering away to eat other farmers' crops. You'd have to weed the gardens and plow the fields and generally keep things in motion.

Isaac: I have been studying motion. Watch. I will tie a string to the apple stem. I can whirl around and around in a circle. This force keeps the apple in motion unless the string pulls loose like it just did. The apple travels in a straight line when it flies off. The force of gravity pulls it to Earth.

John: Always gravity . . .

Isaac: The moon is like the apple. It would fly straight off into the heavens, but it is tied by an invisible string—a force. This force is gravity. So the moon is always ready to fly off and always held in its orbit around Earth.

John: I think you've become moonstruck watching the moon too much.

Isaac: If the apple is moving, and someone hits it with a stick, the apple moves in the same direction of the force. A ball hitting a stick moves in the same direction the stick is moving.

John: *(sarcastically)* No kidding.

Isaac: Watch as I tie the string again. I swing the apple forward. The apple swings back. It works every time. For every action, there is an equal and opposite reaction. This is another law of motion.

Catherine: But what does it mean, Isaac?

Isaac: It means that when you pull an arrow back in a bow, the arrow flies forward. This principle will also help send objects to the heavens.

Edward: I think the sun will turn blue or green before that happens.

Isaac: But it already is multicolored. There are seven colors in the light.

John: I only see yellow or white.

Isaac: I put a hole in my mother's shutters and let in one ray of sunlight so that it hits a triangular piece of glass, a child's toy, which I bought at the town fair last week. The light spread out into a rainbow just like you see after a rain. All seven colors were displayed on the white paper.

Catherine: But the colors come from the glass or the rain, don't they?

Isaac: No, Catherine, the colors are in the white light. There are seven rays of light that together make up white light. I put a mirror and a second glass prism next to the first, and the colors came through the second prism as white light.

Edward: That is very clever, Isaac, I must say. It is almost as wonderful as that mouse-powered windmill you created when you lived with us as a grammar school student. But it isn't any more useful than that toy windmill.

John: The toys I remember best are the kites that Isaac made. It was fun to watch his kites fly in the afternoon wind, but remember those night kites he flew? You put small fires burning in a box on the flying kite. They scared the living daylights out of everybody in town. People were sure they were devils let loose from hell to destroy us.

Edward: Or, omens of the end of the world . . .

Catherine: Isaac, you are still just a child playing with different toys. How will you ever make a living as a farmer if you are always playing with toys? How will you support a wife and children?

Isaac: But Catherine, I will finish college someday, and I will probably be able get some job to pay for own my food and rent.

Catherine: You have a manor here.

Isaac: But the world is full of things I must know. I have been working on the orbits of the planets. I am sure that they are not circles but ovals. I am going to build a telescope so small that I will be able to carry it in one hand. I will see the planets in far greater detail than ever before. Understanding how light works will help me.

Edward: How do you learn these things—like the movements of the moon?

Isaac: By thinking about them all the time, day and night.

Narrator: Isaac Newton went back to college when the plague was over. He became a professor of mathematics and eventually wrote a book called *Mathematical Principles of Natural Philosophy* that included his discoveries about gravity, the laws of motion, and many other scientific ideas. He described his idea of fluxions that are now called "calculus." He was often lonely and even had trouble getting along with close friends. He never married.

READER'S RESPONSE: NEWTON'S APPLE

Directions

- These discussion activities and questions may be used in small groups or with the entire class. They may also be used by the actors as a part of their preparation for the reading.
- Refer to the script "Newton's Apple" when responding to all questions. You may also find useful facts in the background section, biographies, textbooks, and Internet sources.
- Make notes on the lines provided below each question before your group discussion.

General Discussion

1. Which of Isaac's visitors liked Isaac the most and respected what he did? Explain your choice.

   _____
   _____
   _____

2. With which of Isaac's toys or inventions would you have liked to work? Why?

   _____
   _____
   _____

3. Why do you think Newton made so many discoveries?

   _____
   _____
   _____

Making It Personal

Would you like to be a person like Isaac Newton? What would be the good things and the unpleasant things about his life and character? Explain your answer.

   _____
   _____
   _____

What do you think was Isaac Newton's greatest discovery or invention? Explain your choice.

   _____
   _____
   _____

Who do you think was the greatest genius in the history of the world: Isaac Newton, Leonardo da Vinci, or someone else? Explain your choice.

   _____
   _____
   _____

READERS' THEATER

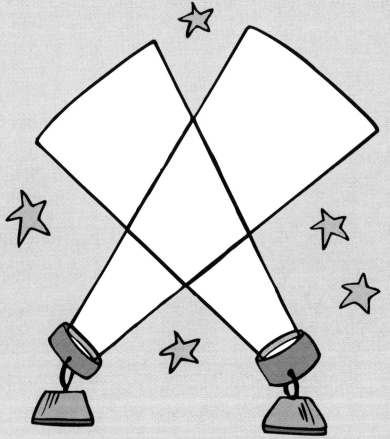

THREE TIMES AROUND THE WORLD

BACKGROUND: THREE TIMES AROUND THE WORLD

Captain James Cook

Captain James Cook was a British officer from a poor family who rose to importance because of his dedication and skill as a sailor. He led three voyages around the world on missions to discover unknown lands and chart water routes through the Pacific Ocean. Cook was a highly skilled navigator and an excellent leader of men. His long voyages added immensely to the store of knowledge about the Pacific Ocean, South Pacific islands, Australia, New Zealand, and the seas near Antarctica. The Polynesian peoples he met and interacted with had been little known before his voyages.

Captain James Cook

The Three Voyages

The first voyage from 1768 to 1771 was officially intended to achieve two purposes. The astronomers on board were to observe the passage of Venus across the face of the sun on June 3, 1769, from the island of Tahiti. Unfortunately, atmospheric conditions prevented clear viewing of Venus. The other objective was to find the Southern Continent that was believed to be a land in the Southern Hemisphere similar to Europe. In his ship, the *Endeavour*, Cook explored the coasts of New Zealand and Australia. In the seas near Antarctica, he encountered massive icebergs and an endless expanse of ice. His ships were battered by violent storms, and his men suffered terrible cold.

The second voyage was intended to find the Southern Continent. Cook had two ships, the *Resolution* and the *Adventure*. This voyage from 1772 to 1775 included a layover in Tahiti and the discovery of the Tongan Islands. He rediscovered the Marquesa Islands and Easter Island. Cook crossed the Antarctic Circle twice looking for the continent. Cook's carefully kept logs proved that it could not exist. He sailed over 70,000 miles of ocean in three years.

The third voyage from 1776 to 1780 was aimed at finding the Northwest Passage, a long-sought-after route from the Atlantic Ocean through North America to the Pacific Ocean. With his two ships, the *Resolution* and *Discovery*, he revisited some of the Pacific Islands and discovered the Hawaiian Islands. He explored the Aleutian Islands, the coasts of Alaska and Russia, and the Bering Strait. Captain Cook was killed in the Hawaiian Islands after a dispute with the natives.

SCRIPT SUMMARY: THREE TIMES AROUND THE WORLD

This script is a discussion between the Secretary of the Royal Society of Britain, which helped sponsor Captain Cook's voyages, and four men who accompanied the captain on his voyages. The men describe some of their adventures of the first voyage, including their journey along the eastern side of Australia and the discovery of the Great Barrier Reef, which almost capsized their ship.

The four men, two officers, a botanist, and an astronomer, explain how Captain Cook was insistent upon protecting his crew from the deadly scourge of scurvy and how he used fruits and vegetables to combat the disease. The men offer many details about the cultural behavior of the Maori, Tahitians, Hawaiians, and other Polynesian peoples that they encountered on the voyages. They describe how cultural misunderstandings led to Captain Cook's death in Hawaii.

The officers and scientists describe their voyages in the frozen southern waters near what is now known to be Antarctica and their efforts to find the nonexistent Southern Continent. They were as unsuccessful in finding the elusive Northwest Passage, which was the focus of the third voyage. The secretary and narrator conclude the script with an evaluation of the importance of these voyages.

Assignment

Read the readers' theater script "Three Times Around the World." Prepare for the performances and share your interpretations of the scripts with the class.

Extensions: Writing and Literature

- Write a script based on one of the events listed below or another one related to the voyages of Captain Cook or the Age of Exploration. Use the background section, books, and Internet sites for ideas.

  Discovering the Great Barrier Reef

  Life aboard one of Captain Cook's ships

  A scene in a Tahitian, Maori, or Hawaiian village

  The death of Captain Cook

  Around the world with Ferdinand Magellan

  Around the world with Sir Francis Drake

  Mutiny on a ship

  Exploring the Antarctic or Arctic waters

- Read *Stowaway* by Karen Hesse. Use one episode or a chapter of this fictional diary of Captain Cook's first voyage as the basis for a readers' theater script about the voyage and the men who made it. After practicing your script, share your performance with the rest of the class.

SCRIPT: THREE TIMES AROUND THE WORLD

This script describes some of the adventures and experiences of the men who three times circumnavigated the globe with Captain James Cook. There are six speaking parts.

Narrator: Captain James Cook was a British sailor who commanded three voyages around the world on missions to discover unknown lands and chart water routes through the Pacific Ocean. The Secretary of the Royal Society for Improving Natural Knowledge, an organization of British scientists, is interviewing four men who sailed with Captain Cook on his voyages.

Secretary: Gentlemen, we are honored to have you here with us today to describe the remarkable achievements that you and Captain Cook made on your three voyages. What were some of the special things you learned and saw on the first voyage?

Joseph Banks: As you know, I was the botanist on the first voyage, and we did discover an enormous number of new plants and creatures of every description. In Australia, we saw kangaroos for the first time. I shot one and we found that it tasted quite good, especially to men who were hungry for the taste of fresh meat.

Captain Clerke: We carefully explored the eastern side of Australia that had never been seen by Europeans before. Captain Cook charted the coast as he did with all of our explorations. You may be absolutely assured that his charts are precisely accurate. If he says land is there, it is.

Joseph Banks: We also discovered the Great Barrier Reef, a huge underground reef made of coral which is over 1,000 miles long. It was magnificent and extremely colorful.

Lieutenant Gore: It almost killed us, too. We discovered the reef when we ran into it and smashed a huge hole in the *Endeavour*. We had to throw much of our equipment off the ship to lighten our load and pump out tons of water. It was a miracle that part of the reef actually stuck in the hole and kept the ship partially afloat.

Joseph Banks: As a plant specialist, I was especially impressed by Captain Cook's determination to keep his crew safe from scurvy. You all know that hundreds of thousands of sailors have died of that dreaded disease. He had heard that certain plants and foods might prevent it. The Captain was forever testing new plants, fruits, and grasses on the crew. We had a large stock of orange and lemon syrups and four tons of sauerkraut, a kind of pickled cabbage. The men hated it at first, but eventually they learned to enjoy it.

William Bayly: The man weren't fond of the Captain's insistence that they eat these foods or keep their quarters clean, but it worked. We all know that some ships have become death ships with every sailor dead from scurvy. The symptoms are clear. Teeth rot and fall out, joints swell, bodies become covered with sores, and men lose the strength to work. They become listless and die. The captain was so strict that he even insisted that sailors keep their hands clean. We never lost a sailor to scurvy. No other ship can make that boast.

Secretary: Indeed. Tell us about the natives you encountered. I know that you had some difficulties with these peoples.

Joseph Banks: The aborigines of Australia were the saddest group we met. They are very primitive. They appear to be nomadic. We got along well with them, but they mostly avoided us; and they were the only people who didn't seem to want to trade for anything we had.

William Bayly: The Maori are one of the many Polynesian tribes we met on our voyages. These natives of New Zealand tattoo their faces and bodies, and they can be very warlike. They immediately came out to our ships with war canoes. At first, they were unwilling to trade and wanted to fight with us as they do with each other. Clans are often at war.

Lieutenant Gore: In one incident, several shots were fired and some Maori tribesmen were killed. We captured three boys and brought them aboard ship, treating them kindly as the captain ordered. Eventually, we made peace with the tribe which you do by touching nose to nose.

Captain Clerke: On our second voyage, ten of our men had a fight with the Maori while searching for provisions on shore. They were killed.

The Tahitians had some strange customs. Women will feed an important chief by putting food in his mouth, but women never eat with the men. Young girls, as young as twelve, are given tattoos over their legs. A really important chief did not walk. He was carried on the shoulders of another tribesman.

Joseph Banks: The Tahitians and most of the other island peoples had one habit that frustrated the captain and really enraged him. They stole.

Lieutenant Gore: They stole everything. It was almost a game to them. They were willing to trade for goods, but they also took everything they could find—nails, food, rowboats, weapons, and clothes. We never understood why they did it, and none of the islanders could ever give us a reason other than that they just wanted to. They didn't steal property from each other—just from us.

Captain Clerke: That was the reason the captain was killed on our third voyage. We discovered the Sandwich Islands that he named for the Earl of Sandwich, who is a great supporter of exploration. The Hawaiians, who inhabit these islands, originally welcomed us with open arms. They threw a huge party. So many Hawaiians sailed out to our ship and climbed aboard that it lifted to one side and almost fell over in the harbor.

William Bayly: The natives seemed to think that Captain Cook was a god named Lono. We arrived just at the time of year when they celebrate his feast. However, a few days after we left, the *Resolution* broke a mast and sprung a leak, and we had to return to the islands. This time the Hawaiians were unfriendly and angry. They stole everything they could. They threw stones at a crew getting fresh water.

Captain Clerke: The natives stole a small boat, and the captain went ashore to protest. He was extremely angry at all the pilferage of our possessions and went almost crazy, as he had on a few other occasions when the natives simply didn't behave honestly. They attacked and killed him.

Lieutenant Gore: We were unable to mount an attack to save him because the men were scattered in many places.

Secretary: Did you have any success in locating a passage from the Atlantic Ocean through North America?

Captain Clerke: Captain Cook sailed into ice fields so thick with icebergs and frozen glaciers that there was no possible passage. I did the same in the months after his death. We did not see anything that might even suggest such as passage.

Secretary: It is interesting that your voyages were so successful, but none of the objectives of the voyages were ever achieved. On your first voyage, you were unable to clearly observe the movement of Venus across the face of the sun because of atmospheric problems. Nothing could be done about that, of course. You did not find the Southern Continent on either voyage, of course, but Captain Cook's careful charting of land and ocean routes clearly indicates there is no such continent. You did not find the Northwest Passage—which probably does not exist, either.

Lieutenant Gore: We did sail farther toward the South Pole than any ship ever has on our first two voyages. We saw endless ice and massive chunks of floating ice higher than some mountains. The voyages through the southern seas searching for that continent were frightening. Ice can tear up ships. It disheartened the men, and the cold was terrible. Only Captain Cook's leadership kept us going.

Secretary: Gentlemen, your voyages with Captain Cook have added immeasurably to our knowledge of the world. It is clear that Captain Cook's explorations were extraordinary, and your success as a crew will long be remembered by Britain and the world.

Narrator: Captain Cook's three voyages mapped a large part of the unknown world and introduced Europeans to several Polynesian cultures on Easter Island, the Society Islands, and Hawaii. Captain Cook respected the cultures and people he met and was generally understanding of the differences between their beliefs and those of his own culture. An unfortunate result of these discoveries was that future conflicts with European sailors and colonial powers were much more violent and led to a mass depopulation of these peoples.

READER'S RESPONSE: THREE TIMES AROUND THE WORLD

Directions

- These discussion activities and questions may be used in small groups or with the entire class. They may also be used by the actors as a part of their preparation for the reading.
- Refer to the script "Three Times Around the World" when responding to all questions. You may also find useful facts in the background section, textbooks, biographies, and Internet sources.
- Make notes on the lines provided below each question before your group discussion.

General Discussion

1. Why do you think the natives of Hawaii, Tahiti, and other islands stole from Captain Cook's ships? Explain your reasoning.

   _____

   _____

   _____

2. What was the most important discovery made on Captain Cook's voyages? Explain your answer.

   _____

   _____

   _____

3. What were Captain Cook's greatest strengths as a ship's commander? Explain your choices.

   _____

   _____

   _____

4. What was Captain Cook's greatest weakness as a commander? Explain your answer.

   _____

   _____

   _____

Making It Personal

Would you like to have gone on one or all of the voyages with Captain Cook? Explain your reasons.

_____

_____

_____

_____

Describe what your feelings would be if you were a native islander who met Captain Cook and his men.

_____

_____

_____

_____

READERS' THEATER

DEATH OF A KING

BACKGROUND: DEATH OF A KING

The French Revolution

During the 1780s France was considered one of the great world powers. France had flexed its military muscle against its rival, Great Britain, by helping Britain's American colonies achieve their independence. However, beneath the surface, France had extremely serious problems. The government was bankrupt. To pay its bills, taxes were raised on the poorest people while the nobility paid no taxes. Harvests were poor and the price of food skyrocketed.

In 1789, rioting spread across the nation. The French army, largely made up of peasants with officers from the nobility, could not be counted upon to end the rioting and enforce the king's orders. The king was forced to call a meeting of the Estates General—representatives from the three classes who made up French society—the nobility, clergy who owned land, and the peasants. In June 1789, when the king refused to respond to the list of peasant grievances, the peasant representatives called themselves the National Assembly, which threatened the power of the king. Gradually, revolution against the king and nobility spread across France.

The Bastille, a fortress prison where many of the king's enemies were jailed, was stormed by a mob in July 1789. Guns and ammunition were taken and the prisoners were released. The National Assembly issued a "Declaration of the Rights of Man and of the Citizen." In October 1789, a mob of starving market women marched on the king's palace in Versailles and forced the royal family back to Paris. In June 1791, the king and his family tried to flee from Paris. They were caught and returned to Paris.

In August 1792, a mob invaded the castle where the king was living, killed all the soldiers of the Swiss Guard, a hired foreign army that was guarding him, and dragged the king and his family to a prison called the Temple. In September 1792, a mob invaded a prison and massacred nobles and other accused enemies of the state. In January 1793, the king was executed on the guillotine, a machine for beheading. The queen was executed in the fall of 1793. The revolution became more violent and radical creating a year long Reign of Terror fed by more than 18,000 executions. In 1799, the French army under the command of Napoleon Bonaparte took control of the government.

SCRIPT SUMMARY: DEATH OF A KING

The setting for this script is the execution of King Louis XVI of France on January 21, 1793. An American reporter is anxious to explain to his readers the causes of the revolution in France and the feelings of the people involved. The shopkeeper is supportive of the goals of the revolution and explains how it came about. The peasant is a *sans-culotte*, one of the thousands of angry and starving people who have participated in riots throughout Paris and the nation.

Madame LaFave is a peasant woman who participated in the women's march on Versailles that forced the king to return to Paris. She is enraged by the behavior of all aristocrats and the king. All of her children have died as a result of the mistreatment of the peasants and the food shortages that have starved the poor. The soldier is also a peasant who revolted against the king and refused to fight against his people.

The characters describe the course of the French Revolution from the calling of the Estates General by the king through a series of riots and revolts against the authority of the king and the privileges of the aristocracy. In the final part of the script, the king is executed on the guillotine, and the peasant characters feel some sense of justice and revenge.

Assignment

Read the readers' theater script "Death of a King." Prepare for the performances and share your interpretations of the scripts with the class.

Extensions: Writing and Literature

- Write a script based on one of the events listed below or another one related to the French Revolution. Use the background section, books, and Internet sources for ideas and suggestions.

    A scene where peasants revolt against the king

    The storming of the Bastille

    The market women storming Versailles

    Food riots in Paris

    The king fleeing from Paris

- Read *A Tale of Two Cities* by Charles Dickens. You may want to use an abridged or illustrated edition—if your teacher approves. Use one episode or a chapter as the basis for a readers' theater script about life during the French Revolution.

- Read *The Scarlet Pimpernel* by Baroness Orczy. You may want to use an abridged or illustrated edition—if your teacher approves. Use one episode or a chapter as the basis for a readers' theater script about life during the French Revolution from the point of view of the nobility.

SCRIPT: DEATH OF A KING

This script is set during the French Revolution when the people of France overthrew their king and became a republic. There are seven speaking parts.

Narrator: In the late 1780s, France went through a massive social upheaval that led to revolution. The nation had been governed by the king and the nobility, but excessive taxes and food shortages led to rioting and the development of a powerful movement to replace the king and the corrupt system of government with one representing the interests of the people. A radical group of revolutionaries took control of the country and began executing many of those who were considered enemies of the new government. On this day, January 21, 1793, King Louis XVI is scheduled for execution in the Place de la Revolution in Paris.

Reporter: Sir, you look like a shopkeeper. I am a newspaper reporter from America. Can you tell me how you feel about the executions of the nobility and now the king? Americans want to understand what is going on here.

Shopkeeper: I could tell you were an American. You dress like Mr. Franklin did when he was here. I'm personally afraid of the wild actions of the Convention, the radicals who now rule France, but the king and the nobility are getting what they deserve. They were both greedy and corrupt.

Peasant: Liberate France forever! Kill the king! The people must rule!

Reporter: Sir, would you explain why you want the king executed?

Peasant: I can see you're an American. You had your revolution against the British king. We're having ours.

Madame LaFave: Let me tell this American about these pampered royals. We die from starvation while the king and his foreign queen were filling their faces with roast beef, chicken, ham, fancy eggs, wine, cakes, and fancy breads. My brother was killed by the king's soldiers as he begged for food for his family at the castle of one of these arrogant aristocrats.

Peasant: They don't hold their head so high now, do they? Look! Another nobleman has lost his head to the guillotine.

Madame LaFave: All of my children are dead. My oldest son died of exhaustion working our lord's land. My boy, Simon, was killed by an aristocrat who didn't like Simon's attitude when his lordship spoke to him. My girls died from sickness before they were ten years old, but mostly because they didn't have enough food to keep up their strength.

Reporter: How did your revolution start?

Shopkeeper: Well, there were bad harvests for several years, and the king's government spent so much money on war and waste that the government was bankrupt.

Peasant: So naturally, the king decided to raise taxes—not from the rich landowners and the other aristocrats, but from the Third Estate. That was the name for the peasants who worked the land and common tradesmen like our storekeeper here.

SCRIPT: DEATH OF A KING (cont.)

Madame LaFave: We peasants couldn't afford to buy bread, much less pay the taxes, so riots broke out.

Peasant: They called us *sans-culottes*. We don't wear the fancy short pants called *culottes* worn by the rich. We refused to work or pay taxes and we rioted. The king had to keep his army constantly on guard. Every time he put down one riot, another occurred someplace else.

Soldier: Regular soldiers like me are just peasants. We were constantly beaten and abused by our officers, who were all aristocrats.

Peasant: Rioters began stealing food from stores, fancy hotels, and some manor homes of the nobility.

Storekeeper: The king was forced to call a meeting of the three groups who made up French society: the nobility, the clergy who owned land, and the peasants. When the king ignored the grievances presented by the peasants, they formed a National Assembly.

Peasant: A month later on July 14, 1789, riots broke out near the prison where the king jailed his enemies. This fortress was called the Bastille. We grabbed forks, guns, staves, knives, and any weapon we could find. We charged the guards and freed the poor wretches kept starving and beaten in those dungeons. Many soldiers refused to fight for the king and came over to the people's side.

Madame LaFave: We women marched on the king's palace in Versailles demanding bread. We took pikes and forks, some borrowed guns from soldiers who didn't want to fire on us, and we even took a cannon. We forced the king to return to Paris. The royals trembled that day. They knew their judgment day was coming!

Storekeeper: The National Assembly issued a Declaration of the Rights of Man and of Citizens. All people were declared free and equal.

Peasant: Liberty! Equality! Fraternity! We are all free! We are all equal! We are all brothers! No more special favors for the royals and the aristocrats! No more titles like "Your Highness" and "Your Lordship." Our only title is "Citizen."

Madame LaFave: Then in 1791, that idiot king and his worthless foreign queen tried to escape from France and join the armies of our enemies. He was caught and brought back to Paris. In 1792, the place where he was being held and guarded by some Swiss Guards, who were paid soldiers, was attacked.

Soldier: I was among the attackers along with many citizens.

Peasant: I was there, too.

Soldier: Those Swiss Guards fought bravely, I'll give them that, especially since they're only hired soldiers. But we beat them and killed every one.

Storekeeper: The king was sentenced to death for crimes against the people.

Madame LaFave: They didn't list all the crimes. There isn't enough paper and ink in all Paris to list the names of the people whose lives he harmed by his actions.

Soldier: There he is! He's next to meet the guillotine. His hands are tied and he's talking.

King: I die innocent of the crimes of which I've been charged. I pardon those who have brought about my death . . .

Madame LaFave: Innocent, my eye! His hands are stained with the blood of my family!

Peasant: Tens of thousands are dead by starvation, mistreatment, imprisonment, or cold-blooded murder.

Narrator: The king put his head beneath the blade, and so his reign was ended!

Madame LaFave: Good riddance!

Narrator: After the death of the king, France was ruled by a series of radical revolutionary groups each more dictatorial and intense in its desire to cleanse France of all things that represented the old regime. Many more aristocrats and others whom the government feared were executed on the guillotine. Eventually, the French army under Napoleon Bonaparte took control of the government.

READER'S RESPONSE: DEATH OF A KING

Directions

- These discussion activities and questions may be used in small groups or with the entire class. They may also be used by the actors as a part of their preparation for the reading.
- Refer to the script "Death of a King" when responding to all questions. You may also find useful facts in the background section, books, Internet, and other sources.
- Make notes on the lines provided below each question before your group discussion.

General Discussion

1. Why did the French people overthrow King Louis XVI?

_____

_____

_____

2. How do you think the American Revolution affected the French Revolution?

_____

_____

_____

3. How was the French Revolution different from the American Revolution?

_____

_____

_____

4. Why do you think the people succeeded in the 1790s in overthrowing the entire system of French government and the dominance of the nobles when the system had existed for hundreds of years?

_____

_____

_____

Making It Personal

How would you have felt if you were a peasant living during the French Revolution? Describe your feelings and reactions.

_____

_____

_____

Toward which character in the play did you feel the most sympathetic? Why?

_____

_____

_____

READERS' THEATER

THE GREAT BALLOON RIDE

BACKGROUND: THE GREAT BALLOON RIDE

Eyes on the Skies

Many efforts have been made by men across the centuries to fly. Early Greek myths, such as the tale of Icarus, envisioned men flapping feathery wings and sailing across the skies. In the late Middle Ages other efforts to create bird-like flying machines were made. Leonardo da Vinci designed several flying vehicles, including the parachute and the helicopter.

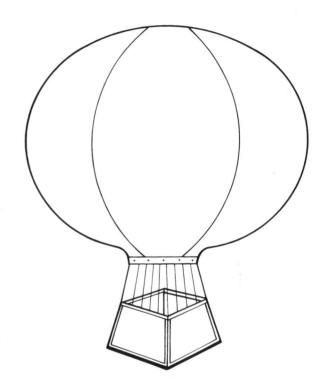

The Montgolfier Brothers

The Montgolfier brothers were born into a family of paper manufacturers in France in the 1740s. There were 16 children in the family, and the father's paper making business was very successful. Of the two brothers, Etienne, the businessman, brought in the latest innovations from France and Holland and made it a very flourishing business. Joseph was the more scientific of the two and had the imaginative and creative mind of an inventor. He observed the effect of embers in a fire rising with the smoke, and that drying laundry over a fireplace caused the material to rise. He came to believe that there must be a kind of gas which he called "Montgolfier gas" that caused the paper and cloth to rise.

The two brothers built several contraptions using fire, light wood, and cloth which flew up several feet. These experiments were conducted in 1782. In 1783, they created a balloon that flew in front of group of dignitaries in the community of Annonay where they lived. They later went to Paris where they built a much larger balloon. They launched this balloon in September with a crew consisting of a duck, a chicken, and a sheep. The flight lasted about eight minutes. The balloon traveled about two miles and reached a height of 1,500 feet.

Success

The great flight occurred on November 21, 1783 with two adventurers aboard. Pilatre de Rozier was a physicist, and Francois Laurent was an army officer and a high-ranking nobleman called a *marquis*. The two men volunteered to fly the balloon, and after initial opposition from King Louis XVI, the inventors and adventurers convinced him that the honor of France and of the king required them to make the flight. The flight was quite successful. They went more than half a mile high and traveled about five miles in 25 minutes. Part of the balloon caught fire during the landing, but the fire was extinguished using sponges and de Rozier's coat. Pilatre de Rozier became the first man in history to die in a manned flight when he unsuccessfully tried to cross the English Channel two years later. Ben Franklin, who was ambassador to France from the United States, witnessed the flight and commented that he, too, hoped to fly in a balloon.

SCRIPT SUMMARY: THE GREAT BALLOON RIDE

The narrator sets the time and place for this script in Paris on November 21, 1793. The Montgolfier brothers, Joseph and Etienne, are determined to launch the first manned, heavier-than-air, hot air balloon flight. They believe they have discovered a gas that lifts the balloon when it is filled with smoke. There are many observers for this momentous event including King Louis XVI and his wife Marie Antoinette, as well as the American ambassador to France, Benjamin Franklin.

Two young adventurers, Pilatre de Rozier, a young physicist, and Francois Laurent, a marquis or count, are determined to make the flight. In a previous trial during the summer, the inventors had sent a duck, a chicken, and a sheep aloft with success. The king is worried about the dangers, but the adventurers and the Montgolfier brothers convince him that the honor of France requires them to be the first to fly. The flight is a great success, traveling for about five miles in 25 minutes. The balloon does catch on fire before it lands, but no one is injured. A crowd of peasants mobs the heroic airmen when the balloon lands.

Assignment

Read the readers' theater script "The Great Balloon Ride." Prepare for the performances and share your interpretations of the script with the class.

Extensions: Writing and Literature

- Write a script based on one of the events listed below, or another one related to the manned flight.

   You are a hidden stowaway on the first hot air balloon flight. Tell the adventure from your perspective.

   A hot air balloon is used on a spy mission during the American Civil War.

   You and your best friend accidentally take off, without your guide on a modern hot air balloon.

   You are Pilatre de Rozier when he tried to cross the English Channel in a hot air balloon.

- Read *Hot Air* by Marjorie Priceman that describes the first flight of the duck, the chicken, and the sheep. Use them as your speaking characters in a script. After practicing your script, share your performance with the rest of the class.

SCRIPT: THE GREAT BALLOON RIDE

This script offers a glimpse of the first manned flight in a hot air balloon. There are 11 speakers. Speakers will also play members of the crowd.

Narrator: The scene is Paris in November 1783. A huge and colorful balloon is being filled with hot air. There is a small basket under the balloon holding two well-dressed young men. The Montgolfier brothers are preparing the balloon for takeoff. King Louis XVI and his queen, Marie Antoinette, and Ben Franklin, the American ambassador to France, are among the many spectators. An air of celebration and expectation fills the crowd.

Young Woman: Pilatre, mon cher, my beloved, don't go. It's too dangerous. I would go mad without you, not seeing your manly face. My heart would be forever lost. I would waste away to nothingness.

Pilatre de Rozier: Mon cher, do not let it trouble your pretty head. I will return safely carrying the glory of France branded on my soul. No power on the earth could keep me from your embrace.

Countess: Francois, my Marquis, you must be reasonable. It is one thing to risk your life as an officer for king and country, but soaring off into the heavens is terribly dangerous. My arms ache to hold you and keep you safe.

Marquis d'Arlandes: Countess, man was meant to explore all the earth and the air above it. It is in our very souls. I will return safely to your arms.

Ben Franklin: I just love the drama of French women in love. They put their entire heart and soul into the idea of "l'amour." They love being in love.

Ambassador: Indeed, my dear Dr. Franklin, we French are concerned with two things: love and good food.

Louis XVI: My dear friend, Monsieur de Rozier, I am truly worried. You have a great future as a scientist. My brave Marquis, I would be shattered if you were lost.

I forbid it!

Montgolfier, stop this instant!

It is too dangerous. It is foolhardy to tempt. Men were not intended to fly.

Marie Antoinette: Indeed, Your Royal Highness. If men should fly, they would have wings.

Countess: Yes, and feathers, too.

Joseph Montgolfier: Your Majesty, please listen. This Montgolfier gas is perfectly safe. We have flown balloons before. You know that we even sent up a chicken, a sheep, and a duck in previous flights.

Louis XVI: The chicken broke his wing, and the other animals were terrified!

Etienne Montgolfier: Your Majesty, most probably the sheep stepped on the chicken out of fright. These brave Frenchmen know no fear.

Ben Franklin: I wonder why the two brothers don't take the first ride. I would love to ride in that contraption.

Ambassador: Indeed, Dr. Franklin. I heard that the boys promised their father they would not fly. It would ruin the family business if they were lost. Perhaps we can arrange a ride, if the king allows them to fly—and if they return alive.

Marquis d'Arlandes: Your Royal Highness, what Joseph Montgolfier says is true. We saw the balloon fly ourselves. The animals were fearful.

We are Frenchmen. We fear neither man nor beast nor sky.

Louis XVI: But you are valued friends. Perhaps I should order two prisoners in jail to volunteer. They would not be missed.

Etienne Montgolfier: Your Highness, the balloon has been filled by heating the air with a fire of straw and wood. The balloon is made of sturdy cotton, lined with paper.

Louis XVI: But you are sending the fire up in the balloon. Paper and cotton burn!

Joseph Montgolfier: True, Your Highness, but the fire is contained in its own cage.

Ben Franklin: Fire is a dangerous element and difficult to control. Fire is always at risk of escaping its cage. I have designed a stove. I know the dangers.

Pilatre de Rozier: Most Royal Highness, we must ascend in this balloon. The honor of France demands it. You are the King. Your glory and fame will be known to all nations. You are France.

Frenchmen must be the first to fly! We must carry your name and your honor through the skies for all the world to admire.

Louis XVI: But of course, you are right, my dear de Rozier. France must be first, and a Frenchman must be the first to fly.

It is ordered.

Let the balloon ascend!

SCRIPT: THE GREAT BALLOON RIDE (cont.)

Narrator: The ropes were loosened and the balloon ascended into the sky. The crowd cheered wildly.

Ben Franklin: It's free! These are the first men ever to fly.

I wish I were with them.

Crowd: Bon voyage! Bon voyage!

Joseph Montgolfier: It's up! It's climbing swiftly!

Narrator: The balloon rose very high into the air to a height of more than half a mile. It moved swiftly through the sky across the French countryside for about 25 minutes. It traveled a distance of about five miles. The Marquis and de Rozier were amazed by the sense of movement and the view from their balloon.

Marquis d'Arlandes: Oh, my goodness! We are aloft! The people look like toy miniatures.

Pilatre de Rozier: Count, can you feel the freedom?

The air is intoxicating!

We are drifting towards the heavens.

Men can fly—and we are the first!

Marquis d'Arlandes: There is one slight problem—the balloon is on fire.

Pilatre de Rozier: Oh, dear! Well, I do not see a big problem. We are heading away from Paris. Let's wait until we are in the countryside to land.

Marquis d'Arlandes: Good idea.

I do hope we can go down slowly. The fire is catching quite quickly now.

Pilatre de Rozier: There's a field with some children. Look at the people in the distance running to catch up. They seem very excited.

Marquis d'Arlandes: Some are waving and shouting, but others are running away as if we were coming to take them from the earth.

Pilatre de Rozier: The fire may scare them.

We're coming down. Just as well. The balloon is really blazing now.

Narrator: They touched down in a pasture and were soon surrounded by a huge crowd racing toward the balloon, while many others raced away in terror. The peasant families who surrounded the balloon helped pull the two men from the basket. Some in the crowd ripped off buttons and scraps of paper and cloth from the burning balloon. Many in the crowd also grabbed bits of cloth from the fliers' clothes.

One in Crowd: I got a jacket!

Second in Crowd: I've got his shirt—well, part of it.

Third: I got a shoe!

Fourth: His scarf!

Fifth: A stocking!

Pilatre de Rozier: We'd best run, my dear Marquis, or we'll have to greet His Majesty without a stitch.

Marquis: Yes, and wouldn't that be a sight!

Narrator: The two daring aviators returned to Paris disheveled and missing some of their clothes but conscious of the fact that they had succeeded in their effort to become the first humans to fly and land safely. Ben Franklin died less than two years later, before he got an opportunity to ride in this new invention. Pilatre de Rozier later became the first flier to die when he tried to cross the English Channel in another hot air balloon.

READER'S RESPONSE: THE GREAT BALLOON RIDE

Directions

- These discussion activities and questions may be used in small groups or with the entire class. They may also be used by the actors as a part of their preparation for the reading.

- Refer to the script "The Great Balloon Ride" when responding to all questions. You may also find useful facts in the background section.

- Make notes on the lines provided below each question before your group discussion.

General Discussion

1. How did the Montgolfier brothers, the Marquis, and de Rozier convince the King to let them fly?

   _____

   _____

   _____

2. Which character in the script did you like best? Why?

   _____

   _____

   _____

3. Hot air balloons were used by armies in several countries including France, and in the U.S. by the Union army during the Civil War. What military advantages might the use of hot air balloons have for an army?

   _____

   _____

   _____

   _____

Making It Personal

Why do you think Ben Franklin wanted to ride in the hot air balloon?

_____

_____

_____

Describe what your feelings might have been if you had ridden in the balloon that day in 1793.

_____

_____

_____

Would you ride in a hot air balloon if you had the opportunity? Why or why not?

_____

_____

_____

READERS' THEATER

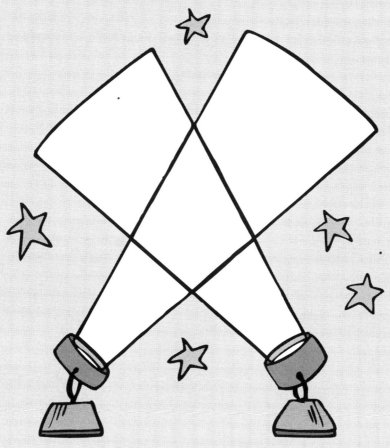

A LASTING IMPRESSION

BACKGROUND: A LASTING IMPRESSION

Impressionism

Impressionism is a style of art that developed in the 1870s in France. The Impressionist painters rejected many of the restrictions of earlier styles of art. They were especially concerned with revealing the impression of what the eye actually sees at a glance. Impressionist artists were concerned with the effect of light on a subject and how it looked to the eye when it is reflected from an object. They used bright colors rather than the duller tones and hues of earlier artists.

Impressionist painters were also influenced by the new interest in Japanese styles of art and by the way the newly invented camera composed a picture. As a result, many of their compositions cut off a part of a subject or showed only a part of a person or object. Impressionists often painted several views of the same subject and often worked outdoors at the site of the subject rather than in a studio. The Impressionists were rarely accepted in the salon exhibitions of traditional painters, so they held eight of their own exhibitions between 1874 and 1886.

Important Impressionists

The name for this style of painting came from an art critic's negative reaction to a painting by Claude Monet called *Impression: Sunrise*. Monet often painted a series of paintings with the same subject. He did thirty views of the cathedral of Rouen and many of his garden.

Claude Monet

Edgar Degas was fond of painting circus performers, ballet dancers, theater performances, and racehorses. He was very influential with several of the Impressionists, but he did not consider himself an Impressionist. Vincent Van Gogh learned from the Impressionists but developed a very unique style. He was unsuccessful in selling his paintings, but they became very popular after his death.

Other major artists of the Impressionist movement were Pierre-Auguste Renoir, Camille Pissarro, Edouard Manet, Gustave Caillebotte, Georges Seurat, Paul Gauguin, and Berthe Morisot, an important woman artist. Mary Cassatt was an American Impressionist who lived in Paris.

SCRIPT SUMMARY: A LASTING IMPRESSION

The setting for this script is a scene in a gallery displaying art for sale by Impressionist painters. A family has come to consider art purchases. Mr. and Mrs. DeFleur are very conservative people who favor traditional styles of art. Their young adult children, James and Monique, are clearly oriented to the new Impressionist art. The gallery director helps explain the intent of the artists.

The family first views some pieces by Edgar Degas that have ballet dancers, racehorses, and circus performers as subjects. The next paintings are cathedral and garden scenes by Monet. The parents' reactions are typically negative. Vincent Van Gogh's famous self-portrait with the severed ear offers insights into his often unbalanced mental state. The family also sees an example of pointillism by Georges Seurat and some works by Mary Cassatt. Neither the older or younger adults have changed their minds about Impressionism as a style. The narrator concludes with information about the enormous influence and success of Impressionism over time.

Assignment

Read the readers' theater script "A Lasting Impression." Prepare for the performances and share your interpretations of the scripts with the class. Study the pictures in the script and try to find reproductions at school, in art books, and on Internet sites.

Extensions: Art and Literature

- Find some reproductions of Impressionistic art. Choose one to use as a model to copy. Use tempera paint, water colors, oil pastel chalks, charcoal pencil, colored pencils, or colored markers for your reproduction. Don't expect to do an exact copy. Do your interpretation of the piece of art.

- Create your own Impressionistic work using any of the media mentioned above. Consider the subject you are going to do and incorporate some feature of the style of the Impressionists: bright colors, concern for light, or unfinished subjects at the edges of the paintings.

- Read *Dancing Through Fire* by Kathryn Lasky. Use one episode or a chapter as the basis for a readers' theater script about ballet in the time of Edgar Degas.

- Read *Linnea in Monet's Garden* by Christina Bjork for information about Monet's life and art. Read biographies of Van Gogh, Monet, Gauguin, or Cassatt. Use the information to create a script about some episode in the artist's life.

SCRIPT: A LASTING IMPRESSION

This script describes the attitudes toward Impressionism in the world of art and culture in the late 1800s. There are six speakers.

Narrator: The world of art and culture in the late 1800s was turned on its ear with the development in France of an entirely new style of painting called Impressionism. The Impressionist artists deliberately rejected the styles and subjects of the old masters of previous centuries. These new artists used bright colors and common people as subjects in natural settings at dances, cafes, parks, and public gatherings. They were intrigued by the effect of light in a painting. Because they were not accepted in the traditional galleries and salons of Paris, they produced their own exhibitions. This scene is set in an art gallery with paintings on display by the Impressionists. A wealthy family has come to view the paintings.

Mr. DeFleur: What kind of gallery is this anyway, James? This art would never be accepted in any decent salon or museum. Would you look at this picture?

James: That's by Edgar Degas, Father. It's an excellent example of the new style.

Gallery Director: Indeed it is. Mr. Degas is very popular at present.

Mr. DeFleur: Why it's not even finished! The artist didn't even plan out his painting. The ballet dancer is half painted on the canvas and half missing.

Monique: It's the new style, Father. He's been influenced by the invention of the camera that doesn't always get everyone completely into a picture. See, in this painting of racehorses, only part of the horses is showing. It's realistic.

Mr. DeFleur: It's ridiculous!

SCRIPT: A LASTING IMPRESSION (cont.)

Mrs. DeFleur: It's disgraceful. What artist is going to paint dancers anyway? There's a painting of a circus performer in midair. They should be painting respectable people.

Gallery Director: Well, our Impressionist artists see the beauty in people from all stations in life—the poor as well as the rich.

Mr. DeFleur: Do you expect the poor to buy art?

Mrs. DeFleur: Look at this collection. The artist did four pictures of the same cathedral.

Mr. DeFleur: Well, a cathedral is an acceptable subject but look how unclear it is. And what are all these fuzzy bright colors about? The air is not watery green and drizzly purple.

Gallery Director: That set is by Claude Monet. He wanted to show the effect of light at different times of the day. The cathedral is shown through the light at a particular time of day. This one is at eight in the morning, the second at ten, the third at noon, and the fourth in the late afternoon.

Mr. DeFleur: Well, what did he do—switch from one painting to another during the day?

Gallery Director: Well, yes, that was the idea. He did a series of thirty paintings of the cathedral at Rouen at different times of day.

Mr. DeFleur: I like my buildings dark and clear. No funny stuff with fuzzy-colored light.

Mrs. DeFleur: This work is by the same painter, Claude Monet.

Gallery Director: Many patrons admire Monet's nature scenes. You might like these lily pads and the garden scenes. He did several with the same subject.

SCRIPT: A LASTING IMPRESSION (cont.)

Mr. DeFleur: That's another painting he couldn't make up his mind about. There's way too much green. His paintings are all fuzzy.

Monique: The painter, Paul Gauguin, left France to get in touch with nature. He went to Tahiti and lived there for years. He painted the people he met there. One of these girls is his Tahitian wife. Of course, he left one in France, too. I wonder how she felt when he returned after being away for years.

Gallery Director: These paintings by Pierre Auguste Renoir celebrate the female form.

James: Their faces and figures suggest grace and beauty.

Mr. DeFleur: This artist had done a portrait of some poor old man who appears to be mad or delusional. What happened to the ear, I wonder?

Gallery Director: He cut it off. It's a self-portrait of the artist, Vincent Van Gogh. Vincent is a little disturbed at times, but his painting is revolutionary.

Mr. DeFleur: Well, I'm not fond of revolutions of any kind in politics or art.

Monique: Why did he cut off his ear?

Gallery Director: He had an angry argument with his friend, Paul Gauguin, so he cut off a part of his ear and gave it to his girlfriend. It made sense to him, I guess. The painting reflects his sense of sadness, don't you think?

Mr. DeFleur: I think he belongs in an insane asylum.

Gallery Director: Oh, he often is. He lives, at times, in an asylum for the indigent. Vincent has trouble selling his paintings. People seem put off by the subjects.

Mr. DeFleur: I don't know what to think, but I do know that no one will ever pay a single franc for such rubbish. Look at this painting! The artist put the paint on so thick you can see the ridges.

Gallery Director: That's by Van Gogh, too. Sometimes he gets excited and puts the paint on with a knife.

Mr. DeFleur: Foolish nonsense! Painting is not done with a knife. I suppose these sunflowers are his, too. Look at all the yellow. It's the type of stuff you'd expect of a child or a madman.

Gallery Director: Yellow is his favorite color. Notice the effect of the light on the flowers.

Mr. DeFleur: Do tell. Would you look at this monstrosity? It's all a bunch of dots. The whole painting is made up of little blobs of color. Couldn't he draw a line?

James: It's by George Seurat, Father. They call this style of art pointillism. He creates his pictures using tiny dots of paint. It's very effective, don't you think?

Mr. DeFleur: I think it's mindless foolishness.

Monique: Do you like these paintings of children?

Mr. DeFleur: Who would paint children in a boat? The children are not even dressed up. They're in play clothes. Who would buy such stuff?

Monique: These paintings are by Mary Cassatt. She's an American artist who works with the Impressionists.

Gallery Director: You can see the influence of Japanese art in this painting by Miss Cassatt.

Mr. DeFleur: Well, women have no business painting anyway, and I have no interest in Oriental art. Look at all those ridiculously bright colors. All of her subjects are women and children. Doesn't she know any important men?

James: Rumor has it that Degas is her boyfriend, sometimes anyway.

Mr. DeFleur: They deserve each other. He paints horses and dancers, and she paints children. Neither of them will ever amount to anything. Nor will any of these other wild-eyed artists. This Impressionism is just a passing fad that will have little effect on the world of art. Come, dear, let's find some art which will stand the test of time and be a desirable investment.

Gallery Director: Thank you for coming.

Narrator: The French Impressionists and their work became an immensely popular and creative force in the history of art. Their paintings are among the most imitated by other artists. Their images and ideas have influenced many of the trends in modern 20th century art. Some of the artists, like Claude Monet and Pierre Auguste Renoir, became very successful during their lives. Vincent Van Gogh sold only one painting in his lifetime, for the price of a loaf of bread. In the century after his death, his paintings sold for millions of dollars.

READER'S RESPONSE: A LASTING IMPRESSION

Directions

- These discussion activities and questions may be used in small groups or with the entire class. They may also be used by the actors as a part of their preparation for the reading.
- Refer to the script "An Ear for Art" when responding to all questions. You may also find useful facts in the background section, art books, and on Internet sites.
- Make notes on the lines provided below each question before your group discussion.

General Discussion

1. Why do you think Mr. and Mrs. DeFleur disliked Impressionistic paintings?

   _____

   _____

2. What appealed to Monique and James about the Impressionistic style?

   _____

   _____

3. What subjects do the Impressionists paint?

   _____

   _____

   _____

Making It Personal

Which Impressionist artist appeals most to you? Why?

_____

_____

_____

Describe what your feelings would be if you were an artist and someone criticized your work.

_____

_____

_____

What kind of art would you like to do: oil painting, sculpture, watercolor, drawing, pastels, origami, or any other? Explain your choice.

_____

_____

_____

READERS' THEATER

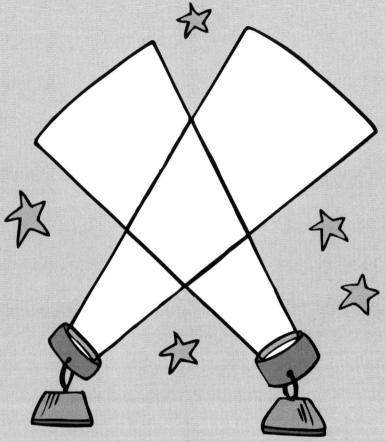

THE COSSACK WINKED

BACKGROUND: THE COSSACK WINKED

The Russian Revolution

The Russian Revolution was one of the most important events in world history. It changed Russia forever in terms of its form of government, industrial power, and international relationships. The revolution was really a movement with several parts.

The March Revolution of 1917

The revolution from March 8th to the 12th began as a protest by women textile workers' against the shortages of food and the high cost of bread. The protest quickly swelled with more workers, students, and soldiers. The crowds grew so large by the third day that virtually all shops, factories, offices, and services were closed. An unpopular and losing war effort, incompetent and ruthless rule by the monarchy, and food shortages fed the rebellion.

The police were overrun by the protesters. Many policemen shed their uniforms and vanished. Police stations were burned and weapons taken. Soldiers ordered to put down the rebellion joined their fellow soldiers in the streets. In desperation, the government ordered the Cossacks to reestablish order. These professional cavalrymen from southern Russia had been the monarchy's enforcers and personal army for hundreds of years. This time, however, the Cossacks did not attack the people. One workman reported that a Cossack had winked at him. This news spread rapidly among the marchers. The Cossacks were with the people this time.

An Unfinished Revolution

On March 15, 1917, just a week after the marches started, Tsar Nicholas II abdicated his throne and a group of labor leaders, Social Revolutionaries, and Communists established a provisional government under the leadership of Alexander Kerensky. This government was unsuccessful in solving Russia's problems. In November of 1917, a revolution by the Bolsheviks, Communists led by Lenin, took control of the government. The Bolsheviks became involved in a five-year-long civil war and a war against other nations to retain control of the nation. By 1922, the Bolsheviks defeated their enemies.

Under Stalin, they established a very autocratic Communist government that was as ruthless in its treatment of its citizens as the old Russian monarchy had been. Russia would go on to become a world power, control many of its neighbors, and eventually have another revolution in the 1990s that brought in some democratic reforms.

SCRIPT SUMMARY: THE COSSACK WINKED

The narrator explains that this script is set at the end of the four days in March of 1917 when the Russian people, especially in the capital, Petrograd, took to the streets to protest food shortages and the war. The correspondent interviews individuals from the marches. The factory worker and the woman marcher explain how severe shortages of bread, the skyrocketing cost of food, and low wages led to marches on March 8th by women textile workers and men in other factories.

The soldier describes the total chaos of war against Austria and Germany and how the inefficient Russian government left men unclothed, barely fed, and inadequately armed to fight much better equipped and organized armies from Europe. He describes how the soldiers joined the workers in their march because there were so many casualties and failures in leadership by the monarchy and its generals. The witnesses tell how the marches were joined by students and other soldiers who were called out to put down the rebellion. They explain why the police had been so hated. Police stations were raided for guns and often burned. The climax came when the tsar's private army of Cossacks, cavalrymen from Southern Russia, are called out and don't attack the people. One workman saw a Cossack wink at him as a sign of support. The word spread that the Cossacks would not attack the people. The monarchy was finished.

Assignment

Read the readers' theater script "The Cossack Winked." Prepare for the performances and share your interpretations of the scripts with the class.

Extension: Writing

Write a script based on one of the events listed below or another one related to the Russian Revolution. Use the background section, textbooks, and Internet sources for additional facts and ideas.

Life on the eastern front for a Russian soldier in World War I

A peasant's life before the revolution

A scene from any of the years of revolution 1917 to 1922

Life in Russia under the Tsar

SCRIPT: THE COSSACK WINKED

This script describes the causes and events of the revolution in March of 1917 that removed the tsar of Russia and radically and forever altered the Russian nation. There are six speaking parts.

Narrator: The Russian Revolution, which begin in 1917 and climaxed with the total victory of the communist forces in 1922, was one of the most important political movements in world history. The tsars had ruled Russia for over 400 years with a remarkable blend of extreme brutality and hapless incompetence. The Romanov dynasty, which had ruled for the last 300 years, sat atop a boiling kettle of peasant unrest and worker frustration. They demonstrated a complete inability to bring Russia into the modern world. Join us as our correspondent interviews some of the participants in a revolution in March 1917 that rocked the world.

Correspondent: Sir, how do you feel about this revolution that is shaking the Russian nation to its foundations?

Factory Worker: I'm part of the uprising. I work in a metal factory here in Petrograd, the capital of Russia. I took to the streets with my fellow workers when the women textile workers left their jobs and marched in protest on March 8. We are not paid enough to buy bread to feed our families. The hours are very long and working conditions are dangerous.

Woman Marcher: Our labor leaders tried to keep us from marching, but we've reached the end of our rope. The cost of bread has gone so high that workers can't feed their families. The markets have little food, and shortages have run the cost beyond what any worker can pay.

Correspondent: What do you want to change?

Factory Worker: The bosses are cruel and impossible. We want trade unions to protect the rights of the workers, a minimum wage that could not be cut by the owners, a shorter workday, and fair treatment by supervisors. The workers should be the bosses and run the factories themselves.

Woman Marcher: We wanted the government to change. I carried a banner reading: "The Monarchy must go." The people must take charge of the nation, or we will all die of war and starvation. My fellow marchers carried signs reading: "We want bread!" and "Down with the War!"

Student: We students joined the marches held on the 9th and 10th. In other revolts, the authorities beat down workers or peasants and kept us isolated. This time we came together in this city and the nation joined us. The marches and strikes were much larger on the 9th and 10th. This time, we will not be stopped.

Correspondent: Why is the Tsar hated?

Student: The Romanov monarchy has always been brutal and incompetent, but this tsar is especially dense. He went to the front to be with his armies, although he knows nothing of war, and left his German-born wife to run the government. She is both stubborn and not too smart. She picked old, weak, and incompetent ministers who could not fix the problems caused by war and starvation. They didn't even pretend to have answers. The Russian people have always suffered. They have always endured. The monarchy expected the same.

Woman Marcher: She let this madman, Rasputin, make decisions about the people she chose and the conduct of the war. This bearded lunatic had convinced the royal couple that he could cure their son of a disease, hemophilia, which means he could bleed to death from even a small cut. Rasputin controlled their minds. Finally, a prince assassinated him, but the damage he did to public confidence could not be repaired.

Correspondent: How did the war affect this revolution?

Soldier: Tsar Nicholas and his advisors went to war without any serious planning. They never seemed to realize that Russia is a very backward nation of peasant farmers fighting against modern, industrialized nations. I was sent to the front when we went to war against Austria.

Correspondent: What were conditions like there?

Soldier: We were a bit lucky with the Austrians. It was still awful. There was very little food because supplies didn't get transported to the front. Farms that the soldiers marched through were stripped bare of every edible thing. We froze because there were not enough coats or warm clothes for the troops. Many soldiers had no boots, and some went into battle barefoot. We lost more troops to hunger, cold, disease, and infections than to the enemy—but the Austrians weren't much better equipped.

Correspondent: How did that change?

Soldier: When the Germans brought their troops to the eastern front, it changed things totally. They were well equipped and had modern vehicles and the military organization to move four divisions into a battle while we struggled with one. Our leaders were poorly organized, and our armies were commanded by officers who were political hacks and incompetent aristocrats. They knew nothing of modern warfare. The Germans were professionals, and they were well equipped and well armed.

Correspondent: Didn't you have weapons?

Soldier: Newly arrived soldiers had to share guns, and many soldiers only had a few bullets for each day. We didn't even have machine guns and the enemy did. The battles sometimes lasted for days. Many of our soldiers died uselessly. One third of our men, especially new recruits, had no guns. They waited until a soldier died to get his weapon. We lost millions of dead, wounded, and captured soldiers due to the incompetence of the generals. Tsar Nicholas went to the front to oversee the war effort. What does he know of war?

Correspondent: Why did the soldiers join the marches in the capital city?

Soldier: We were so overcome by the enemy and our own lack of food, clothes, and supplies that tens of thousands of soldiers simply deserted. Hundreds were shot or whipped for desertion, but it didn't make a difference. We had nothing to lose. My entire battalion simply deserted one night. The roads back to our home in Petrograd and other cities were clogged with wounded soldiers, deserters, starving men, and roving bands of thugs. Russia had become a nation of horrors. I joined the workers and other soldiers because the war must end.

Student: The war actually caused this revolution, I think, so maybe it was a good thing. They took the able-bodied peasant men from the farms and factories to fight the Germans. This left the farms without enough men to harvest the crops in the summer or plant new crops in the spring. The government thought they were going to win the war with their massive numbers. Human bodies are no match for artillery and machine guns.

Factory Worker: The farmers couldn't grow or harvest enough food. The soldiers starved. The workers in the cities couldn't afford to buy food at the inflated prices. The only people eating well or not really affected by the war were the nobility who could afford to live as they always had, on the backs of the poor.

Correspondent: Did this revolution have a leader?

Woman Marcher: No. On March 8th, workers marched along with some soldiers who had deserted from the war. The army was called out and told to fire into the crowds to end the march. Some soldiers did as their officers told them, but many just refused to fire.

Soldier: We called out to our brother soldiers, and many of them simply joined us with their weapons. We broke open some barracks and got other arms.

Correspondent: What about the police?

Woman Marcher: On the second day of the uprising, the police had been ordered to end the rebellion. The police are the most hated people in any Russian city. They beat and kill people without any restraints. They are not going to be punished, and their orders are to break up any marches or rallies immediately using whatever force they need; but this time they had a problem.

Soldier: Many of our men had seen death and terrible things at the front. We had some guns, too. Even though the police killed several of our marchers, the people simply overran and raided the police stations and jails. We released the poor wretches being imprisoned there and took all the weapons we could find. We burned the police stations, too.

Correspondent: What happened with the Cossacks, the tsar's private army?

Factory Worker: The Cossacks have been the protectors of the tsars forever. They are brutal warriors from southern Russia who have ridden their horses over the people in every uprising in Russian history.

Student: The Cossacks have always had special privileges and earned them by beating down rebellions under every tsar. They are cavalrymen who use sabers, pistols, and heavy clubs called "knouts" to whip the peasants and the workers whenever there has been a revolt against the monarchy.

Soldier: On the second day of the marches, the Cossacks were given the order to attack, and they rode their huge horses into the crowd. But they didn't attack the people this time. They held their weapons at the ready, but only a few people were actually hit.

Factory Worker: Then a miracle happened. A mounted Cossack winked at one of our men as he rode his horse down the street. The word spread like wildfire across the crowds on the second day of the strike that the Cossacks would not fight.

Student: Then the Cossacks drove off some policemen who were attacking the crowd. The word spread that the Cossacks were favoring the workers. This was the true moment the monarchy was over. Without the Cossacks, the entire ruling class was defenseless against the people.

Narrator: The marches continued for four days. The groups of labor unions, social revolutionaries, and communist organizations, which had been planning for a revolution in the future, found themselves in charge of a caretaker government. Tsar Nicholas II abdicated on March 15, 1917. Later in November 1917, one group of Communists, the Bolsheviks, would gain control of the government and eventually control Russia by 1922.

READER'S RESPONSE: THE COSSACK WINKED

Directions
- These discussion activities and questions may be used in small groups or with the entire class. They may also be used by the actors as a part of their preparation for the reading.
- Refer to the script "The Cossack Winked" when responding to all questions. You may also find useful facts in the background section, textbooks, and Internet sources.
- Make notes on the lines provided below each question before your group discussion.

General Discussion
1. List the causes of the Russian Revolution in March of 1917.

_____

_____

_____

_____

_____

_____

2. What do you think was the most important reason the Russian people rebelled against their tsar? Explain your answer.

_____

_____

_____

_____

_____

_____

3. The Cossacks had always defended the tsars and attacked any opponents of the monarchy. Why did they support the people this time? Explain your answer.

_____

_____

_____

_____

_____

4. Would the revolution have succeeded if the soldiers had not joined the marchers? Explain your answer.

_____

_____

_____

_____

_____

Making It Personal

How was the Russian Revolution different from the American Revolution? Explain your answer.

_____

_____

_____

_____

_____

Describe what your feelings would be if you had been a Russian soldier, worker, or peasant during the marches.

_____

_____

_____

_____

_____

_____

_____

READERS' THEATER

CRYSTAL NIGHT

BACKGROUND: CRYSTAL NIGHT

The Holocaust

The holocaust is the term used to describe the efforts of the Nazi leaders in Germany to wipe out the Jewish people. More than six million Jews were killed, most of them in slave labor concentration camps run by the German government. The holocaust was a deliberate, organized killing of a people because of their race, religion, or political group.

Choosing a Scapegoat

After the armistice that ended World War I, many Germans were looking for a scapegoat, someone to blame, for their failure to defeat France and England during the war. Because some of the Jews were successful businessmen and belonged to a different religion than the Christian majority, they became an easy target to blame for all of the failures of the nation at war and the terrible economic cost after the war. For centuries in Europe, Jews had been easy targets of envy and anger.

Harassment and Humiliation

The rise of the Nazi party in Germany was fostered by these hatreds. When Hitler came to power in Germany in 1933, a key element of his program was public, legal mistreatment of Jews. The Nazi leaders began with small harassments and minor actions designed to goad on their own followers and abuse the Jews who had no place to seek help. The Nazis controlled the police, the courts, and the machinery of government.

Adolf Hitler

Krystallnacht (Crystal Night)

On the night of November 9, 1938, the Nazis began a new offensive against their Jewish citizens. A Jewish teenager had shot a German embassy official two days earlier in Paris. The Nazi authorities used this as a pretext to encourage widespread rioting, assault, and murder against Jews throughout Germany. Homes were invaded and shops were destroyed. Synagogues were burned and over 90 Jews were murdered. It was the beginning of a brutal effort to remove all Jewish citizens and send them to concentration camps. The Jews called the night "Crystal Night" because so much glass was broken that the streets were literally covered with broken shards of glass.

SCRIPT SUMMARY: CRYSTAL NIGHT

Krystallnacht, or Crystal Night, is the name Jews gave to a night of rioting by mobs of German Nazis who attacked and killed Jews on the streets, destroyed their businesses, and burned their places of worship called synagogues. The script tells the story of five young Jewish teens caught up in the violence and destruction of that terrible night of November 9, 1938.

Sixteen-year old Hannah and her older brother, Daniel, are on their way home when they see the looting and encounter mobs of roving Nazi thugs. They run for their lives from one gang of thugs who grab them, but they pull loose and run into their friends Jacob and Rosa. All four teens escape down an alley. The teens are hiding in a narrow opening between buildings and observe the chaos of burning buildings, screaming victims, and the howling screams of the Nazi thugs who are careening down streets chasing Jews and beating up anyone they can find.

Daniel sees that the mob has grabbed his friend, Erica, and he races out to rescue her telling Jacob to get his sister home safely. The other three children ignore his instructions and rush to help Erica, too. The rioters are startled by the attack of the four teens who help Erica escape. The teens run down a narrow street and hide beneath a cellar door. They then realize that Daniel did not escape. Jacob tells them they have to hide and keep the girls safe. That is what Daniel would want.

The narrator concludes the script with the information that this night that witnessed over 90 murders and widespread destruction was the real beginning of the organized German effort to send Jews to the concentration camps.

Assignment

Read the reader's theater script "Crystal Night." Prepare for the performances and share your interpretations of the scripts with the class.

Extensions: Writing and Literature

- Write a script based on one of the events listed below or another one related to the treatment of Jews or other oppressed minorities during World War II.

    Life in a Jewish ghetto during the Nazi occupation of Poland

    Life for a Jewish family in Germany or an occupied country

    Life and death in a Nazi concentration camp

- Read *The Devil's Arithmetic* by Jane Yolen. Use one episode or a chapter as the basis for a readers' theater script about life in a Nazi concentration camp. (**Note to Teacher:** Review material in the book prior to classroom study.)

- Read *The Diary of a Young Girl* by Anne Frank or *Malka* by Mirjam Pressler. Use one episode or a chapter as the basis for a readers' theater script about life hiding from the Nazis.

SCRIPT: CRYSTAL NIGHT

There are 6 speaking parts in this script. Performers can do the rioters' lines as a group.

Narrator: Krystallnacht, or Crystal Night, is the name German Jews gave to the night of November 9, 1938, when mobs of Nazi Party members and their supporters went on a rampage throughout Germany. A Jewish teenager shot a German embassy official in Paris two days earlier resulting in the German's death. This incident was used as a pretext throughout Germany to attack Jews on the streets, to loot and burn their shops, and to burn synagogues. Hannah is a 16-year-old Jewish girl on her way home with her older brother, Daniel, when they are caught in the riot. Jacob and Rosa are their friends.

Hannah: Daniel, we have to get home. The Nazis are everywhere. Our parents are going to be worried. There are mobs on every street.

Daniel: We must be careful. The mobs are looking for anyone. Oh, look at Stein's bakery! The crowd is smashing the windows and looting the place. Those thugs aren't even stealing things to use. They're just throwing the food into the street and destroying the tables and chairs.

Hannah: Why do they hate us so? We never did anything to earn such hatred.

Daniel: They need someone to blame when things go bad. We Jews are good targets. We're easy to recognize, easy to blame, and convenient targets for their loathing. Oh, no! They see us!

Rioters: Jews! Get them! Get those Jews!

Narrator: Hannah and Daniel run for their lives back down the street and run right into a pair of thugs with their hands full of loot. One of the men grabs Hannah, and Daniel fights with him trying to get his sister free. She rips loose from his grasp leaving the rioter with a handful of her dress.

Daniel: Run, Hannah! Run!

Hannah: No! Let my brother go!

Rioters: There they are!

Narrator: Hannah kicks one of the thugs in the leg. Daniel pulls loose, grabs his sister's hand, and they run down the street, with both groups of rioters in hot pursuit. All of a sudden they turn a corner and see their friends and neighbors, Jacob and Rosa.

Jacob: This way. Through the alley! Run!

Narrator: The four young Jews race madly down the alley with the mob still in pursuit. All of a sudden, Jacob turns into a narrow space between buildings and leads them to another street. The mob rushes by still looking for victims.

Jacob: The Nazis are wandering the streets grabbing every Jew they can find. They burned my father's printing shop.

Rosa: They looted my father's jewelry store, smashed his cases, and beat him up. Dad told us to go home and take care of our mother.

Jacob: Listen to that howling. Let's see what they're doing.

Narrator: The young Jews quietly look around the corner of the alley they are in to see what's happening on the street to cause such screaming.

Daniel: That's my friend, Erica. I'm going to help her. Jacob, get Hannah home safely!

Narrator: Daniel runs screaming down the alley toward the startled rioters. Jacob, Hannah, and Rosa run after him rather than away. Daniel barrels into the rioters and kicks the one holding Erica. The distraction allows Erica to tear loose from the men holding her. Jacob hits a rioter, and Hannah and Rosa grab Erica and flee back down the alley. Jacob races off behind them.

Jacob: There's a hiding place just before the next street! Turn left! Follow the wall of the building. There's the entrance to the cellar. Help me lift the cellar door. Squeeze in! Hurry! I can hear them coming!

Narrator: The young people lift the cellar door and slide down through steps into a cellar below an apartment building.

Erica: *(Whispering)* Daniel, thank you. Thank you, Hannah! Daniel . . . Daniel?

Jacob: Sssh, Erica! Daniel didn't get away. They held onto him.

Erica: We've got to go help him. Let me out!

Hannah: I'll go with you.

Jacob: No, girls. Daniel knew what he was doing. His fighting and yelling distracted the mob. Maybe he'll get lucky and escape if the mob gets distracted. He wanted you girls safe. We'll stay here for the night and try to make it home in the daylight. Our parents will be frantic, but it's our only chance.

Narrator: The Jews called this event Krystallnacht, or Crystal Night, because so much glass was broken in the night of rioting. It was a major step in the Nazi war against the Jews. Over 90 Jews died as a result of Crystal Night. Jews were no longer just harassed and abused. The Nazis soon began rounding up and deporting Jews to the concentration camps.

READER'S RESPONSE: CRYSTAL NIGHT

Directions

- These discussion activities and questions may be used in small groups or with the entire class. They may also be used by the actors as a part of their preparation for the reading.
- Refer to the script "Crystal Night" when responding to all questions. You may also find useful facts in the background section.
- Make notes on the lines provided below each question before your group discussion.

General Discussion

1. Why is the story called "Crystal Night"?

_____

_____

_____

_____

_____

_____

2. Why did some Germans hate the Jews?

_____

_____

_____

_____

_____

_____

3. Have there been any times in American history when minorities in this country have been threatened by mobs? What caused these episodes of violence to Asians, African-Americans, Native Americans, Irish-Americans, and other groups?

_____

_____

_____

_____

_____

_____

Making It Personal

How would you have felt if you were a Jew caught in the violence of Crystal Night?

_____

_____

_____

_____

_____

_____

How would you react if you witnessed mobs running wild like they did on Crystal Night? Explain your answer.

_____

_____

_____

_____

_____

_____

Have you ever heard of or seen behavior in school or your community toward people based on differences of race, language, or culture? Describe what happened.

_____

_____

_____

_____

_____

_____

_____

_____

.

Made in the USA
Columbia, SC
27 June 2022

62363905R00063